Life on the Spectrum is a masterpiec[e]
stuck, or frustrated with the daily demands and difficulties of raising a
child on the Autism Spectrum, this is a MUST READ! These stories
are real and raw, written with unabashed honesty and unashamed
human fragility. Every page offers a new, hope-filled perspective that
will keep you moving forward. You will find refreshment...a renewed
sense of peace and purpose as you care for those struggling with
spectrum disorders. Each chapter ends with thought-provoking
questions, leading you to find God's help and hope as you lean into His
sovereign care. More than anything, you will feel understood because
these folks have been exactly where you are today.

COLLEEN SWINDOLL-THOMPSON

> Mother of an adult with autism and other disabling conditions
> Director of Reframing Ministries, Insight for Living

Parents of kids with autism all too often find themselves isolated and
alone - isolated from friends, family and church. The authors of *Life on
the Spectrum* have experienced it all. Their stories of confronting and
overcoming the challenges common to families impacted by disability,
shared from a Christian worldview, provide hope, encouragement and
inspiration. This book is a wonderful gift to anyone caring for a child
with autism.

STEPHEN GRCEVICH, MD

> President and Founder, Key Ministry and Author of *Mental
> Health and the Church*

Thoughtfully, and honestly finding and holding on to what is good,
these vignettes will draw you in to the life experiences of families
affected by special needs, with true stories of pain and celebration. This
book will introduce the reader to real stories, giving us an opportunity

to develop a deeper understanding, a reminder that each of us is not alone in this journey and inviting a greater compassion for families among us who have at times been misunderstood or rejected, even by the Church. I am grateful for the vulnerability revealed in these stories of life with a child with a disability.

PAM HARMON

Executive Director, Young Life Capernaum

Heartfelt, transparent, and moving, *Life on the Spectrum* is a devotional resource full of compassion and understanding for the parent of a child with autism. Written by parents of children on the spectrum, their stories share an honest struggle to find support and understanding for their children within the church, in their communities, and even with themselves in the midst of autism's daily challenges. It is a book clearly meant to come along side those who need to know they are not alone and to remind them, regardless of the struggle, we share the same hope in God who is on the journey with us all.

ANITA LUSTREA,

Author, Spiritual Director and host of Faith Conversations podcast

Life on the Spectrum
Faith. Hope. Love. Autism.

Deborah Abbs, Kelli Ra Anderson and Kevin R. O'Brien

with

Kathleen Deyer Bolduc, Michele and Rick Bovell,
Barbara K. Dittrich and Michael Abbs

Foxburrow Media

Treading the Dawn

Copyright © 2018 Deborah Abbs, Kelli Ra Anderson and Kevin R. O'Brien

A joint publication of Foxburrow Media and Treading the Dawn

All rights reserved. No part of this publication may be reproduced, distributed, or transmitted in any form or by any means, including photocopying, recording, or other electronic or mechanical methods, without the prior written permission of the publisher, except in the case of brief quotations embodied in critical reviews and certain other noncommercial uses permitted by copyright law.

Cover design by Barry Smith
Edited by Ellen Vosburg
Copyedited by Janet Kotynski

Scripture quotations marked NLT taken from the *Holy Bible*, New Living Translation, copyright © 1996, 2004, 2015 by Tyndale House Foundation. Used by permission of Tyndale House Publishers, Inc., Carol Stream, Illinois 60188. All rights reserved.

Scripture quotations marked RSV are taken from the Revised Standard Version of the Bible, copyright © 1946, 1952, and 1971 by the division of Christian Education of the National Council of the Churches of Christ in the United States of America. Used by permission. All rights reserved.

Scripture quotations marked NIV are taken from the Holy Bible, New International Version, ® NIV.® Copyright © 1973, 1978, 1984, 2011 by Biblica, Inc.® Used by permission. All rights reserved worldwide.

Scripture quotations marked ESV taken from *The Holy Bible*, English Standard Version. ESV® Text Edition: 2016. Copyright © 2001 by Crossway Bibles, a publishing ministry of Good News Publishers.

Scripture quotations marked NASB taken from the New American Standard Bible Copyright © 1960, 1962, 1963, 1968, 1971, 1972, 1973, 1975, 1977, 1995 by The Lockman Foundation

Scripture quotations marked CEV are taken from the Contemporary English Version, Copyright © 1995 by American Bible Society

Scripture quotations marked GNT are taken from the Good News Translation (GNT) Copyright © 1992 by American Bible Society

Scripture quotations marked TLB are taken from The Living Bible copyright © 1971 by Tyndale House Foundation. Used by permission of Tyndale House Publishers Inc., Carol Stream, Illinois 60188. All rights reserved.

ISBN: 978-0-692-18285-7 (Paperback)

Library of Congress Control Number: 2018957303

www.lifeonthespectrumbook.com

To all of the families struggling with the realities of Life on the Spectrum. It is not easy, but we remain persuaded that nothing — not even the realities of autism — can separate us from the love of God.

TABLE OF CONTENTS

FOREWORD

"If you've met one person with autism, you've met one person with autism."

– Dr. Stephen Shore

As parents of children whose needs, behaviors and life trajectory are different from everyone else's, our parenting journey can be lonely and isolating: an experience few truly understand.

Our children may present with a wide spectrum of abilities, strengths and needs. But we parents are on a spectrum, too: from the fresh terror of a diagnosis to coming to terms with our child's adulthood -- and inevitable future without us; from processing our grief to transitioning to emotional healing; from coping to hoping; from the blessing of abundance in resources and supports to the spiritual blessing of never having enough, yet leaning on the sufficiency of Christ; from teaching and supporting our children to realizing they teach and transform us; from despising autism as a curse to cherishing our children as gifts and blessings, exactly as they are.

As unique and far-ranging as our experiences may be, we also share universal struggles: practical matters of IEP advocacy, special diets, protocols, schedules and appointments, the unrelenting constraints of limited finances and resources, the stress on our marriages while juggling the needs of siblings, and rude comments from ignorant strangers while we manage triggers and meltdowns, including our own.

1

Deeper still, we ask, Why? Why did this happen? Why our child? Why us? Our experience may be one of dashed hopes and expectations, spiritual disillusionment, comparison and envy, estrangement and forgiveness, grief and loss, fatigue and frustrations, fear of the future, navigation of friendships, strained relationships (or bemoaning the lack thereof). Our lifestyle is one where we toggle daily between "love and loss; wonder and fear."

Our children may have special needs. But we do, too.

"Parents of autistic kids get to tell the best stories." writes author Kevin O'Brien. Despite their own stresses of autism-parenting, the contributors of *Life on the Spectrum* have banded together to share their hard-fought-and-won wisdom with you. They have discovered the reality of God's sustaining grace, *through* all the mess and mystery.

Through their stories --nay, testimonies-- that comprise *Life on the Spectrum*, I pray you find someone who "gets" you. Your pain, struggle, and confusion--conjoined with undying love, passion and devotion for your child-- qualify you as part of this wondrous fellowship of shared Otherness.

No matter where you are in your journey, no matter your current spiritual address, you are not alone. Ultimately, *Life on the Spectrum* points us to the only One who truly gets us; the One who has and keeps us in the palm of His mighty hand. Whether we acknowledge Him or not, the Lord is our Master 1:1 shadow aide. He never leaves or forsakes us. Our counselor, protector and provider, the Lord is ever present help in times of trouble. As we strive to maximize our child's potential, our Heavenly Father is striving to maximize ours.

Our prayer is that you would find hope, help and company for the journey. What the enemy intended for harm, God can redeem and repurpose into a blessing. Let us marvel at the spectrum of blessings that *Life on the Spectrum* can bring.

Encased in His grace,

Diane Dokko Kim

Jeremy's undone mum, author of *Unbroken Faith: Spiritual Recovery for the Special Needs Parent*

PREFACE

Our Journey Together

This book began as one of the way-too-many ideas that never stop buzzing around in my brain. The amazing thing, however, is that this idea was different; this idea was one of the few that stuck and actually came to be.

I had just finished reading *Cold Tangerines* by Shauna Niequist. I loved how God spoke to me through the collection of short, organic stories and thought how cool it would be to have a book specifically written to encourage parents like myself, who have a child on the autism spectrum. A selection of short, real-life stories to remind them that they're not alone: *Life on the Spectrum*.

I belonged to a writers' group led by my friend Kelli Ra Anderson, who also has two sons on the spectrum. I told her about my idea, and when I asked if she was interested in writing it together, she agreed. Kevin O'Brien, another friend and writer with a child on the spectrum, joined us soon after. Together, over tacos during lunch breaks and late-night coffee at dining room tables, we prayed and fleshed out the project. We invited other parents with children like our own—or in two cases, the same children—to join the writing team, five signed on, and the book came alive.

As everyone living with someone on the spectrum knows, life can be one wild ride, but we can face its sudden drops and crazy loops so much easier when we know there are others on the same ride. That we are together in this journey. At times we may feel like God has forgotten us in the midst of the day-to-day struggle, but the truth is that God is always with us. He loves us. And He loves our families.

Life on the Spectrum is a collection of honest spiritual reflections from each of us as parents, representing our individual Christian faith perspectives and experiences with children of various ages and degrees of ability. Each vignette, beginning with a Bible verse and concluding with discussion questions, takes a candid, personal look at the challenges we face and celebrates our families' unique victories, letting us laugh at situations others might not understand, and sometimes cry over shared losses and grief.

Whether you are reading this on your own or with a group of friends, we pray God uses it to remind you to find your hope in Christ and that it also lets you know you are in good company on this journey.

Blessings on you and your families,
Deborah Abbs

Oh, one final note. This project was started a long time ago now. In some cases the individual chapters are four or even six years old so you should know that all ages were accurate when the chapter was written.

The Comparison Game

DEBORAH ABBS

I know what it is to be in need, and I know what it is to have plenty. I have learned the secret of being content in any and every situation, whether well fed or hungry, whether living in plenty or in want. I can do all this through him who gives me strength.

Philippians 4:12-13, NIV

While I was playing tennis with a friend, I just could *not* focus on the game. My eyes kept creeping to the people playing on nearby courts as I watched how good they were. I thought, *Wow, look at that woman's backhand. It's so much better than mine. Remember when your serve used to be that fast? What happened to it?*

As I rehearsed all this negative self-talk in my head, I failed to play my best game or even enjoy playing like I usually do. On top of all that, I was almost clobbered by a tennis ball during our warm-up because I wasn't paying attention!

Instead of playing tennis, I played a different but equally popular game: the comparison game. The comparison game is never fun, but it's oh-so-easy to fall into. The rules of this game are simple. Notice how much easier, better, or more right everything is outside yourself and your own life, and compare it to how terrible, bad, or wrong your own situation is.

I hate to admit how often I wind up playing this game, especially since God's Word tells me to be thankful for what He has given me, instead of comparing myself or my family to others.

7

When this game involves my nine-year-old son Luke, who has autism and is mostly nonverbal, it can get downright nasty. Luke was diagnosed with autism right when he turned three, and we were devastated.

No mother ever wants her child to suffer. And autism can feel so dark and lonely sometimes. On the upside—at the time—Luke was diagnosed on the mild end of the spectrum. He talked, not with typical sentences or vocabulary for his age, but with around seventy-five individual words and some two-word phrases. Right away, we placed him in behavioral therapy called Applied Behavioral Analysis and had high hopes he would make progress between this and special education preschool. Instead, by the time he was three and a half years old, he had mostly lost his ability to speak. We hear from him now only on rare occasions. When he is extremely upset, we often hear, "NO!" While we'd love to hear a positive word from him, we are extremely happy to hear the no. It's just good to hear his voice.

To say the least, things have not gone according to what we wanted for Luke. In our better moments, we still trust that the Lord has good plans for Luke, with or without speech. But it's tough. It's tough when my older son Brandon, who is fourteen, wonders, "Will Luke ever get the word brother back?" (He usually says *bruder*.) It's tough when we can't figure out what Luke wants, and he lashes out at us in frustration.

On the other hand, our ten-year-old nephew Teddy, who is also on the spectrum, speaks quite well. He also loves to read and navigate on his iPad—all things Luke is still working on. After spending time with Teddy, I often pray, asking God, "Why? Why can't Luke do the things that Teddy can? Why can't he at least be able to talk more?" I'm off and running as the comparison game begins anew. I wind up my pity party and end up feeling really bummed out and sorry for Luke, and myself. Not only am I unable to love Luke for who he is, I also cannot show excitement about Teddy's progress.

I know this comparison game does nothing positive for Luke, me or the rest of our family. So how do I stop this unhealthy thought pattern? I turn to God's Word, and particularly I read these words from Philippians that I have repeatedly underlined in my Bible: "Let your gentleness be evident to all. The Lord is near. Do not be anxious about anything, but in every situation, by prayer and petition, *with thanksgiving,* present your requests to God. And the peace of God, which transcends all understanding, will guard your hearts and your minds in Christ Jesus." (Philippians 4:5-7, NIV, emphasis added).

We worship an awesome God, and these verses bring me such encouragement. When I compare my situation to someone else's, I feel anxious. Through Paul's writing in Philippians, God commands me not to be anxious because He has a much better way. Paul says to pray and present our requests to God because that is where I will find the peace I want. So that's what I need to do. I must pray with thanksgiving. I need to *be thankful.* Thankful for little things, like Luke's awesome smile that can light up the whole block, and how affectionate and cuddly he is lately. I must be thankful for Teddy's progress, too. When I am thankful, God's Word says *His peace* will guard my heart and mind. Plus, when I'm praying and focusing on being thankful, I have much less time to play the comparison game!

I also find it helpful to compare down instead of comparing up. For example, it's so natural for me to walk into a friend's mansion-sized house and compare it to my average-sized home. Instead, why not think back to my time overseas in eSwatini (formerly Swaziland), Africa, where having electricity and a small apartment means that you are rich? (It would be tough to go on a mission trip to Africa these days. So far we haven't had the guts to get Luke on a plane, since he hates sitting or being restrained.) Instead of comparing, I could volunteer with my church to help pack meals at Feed My Starving Children and be reminded that many children and families live without food. Yes, I bet I can swing that and focus on helping others with less, instead of focusing on those who have more.

I don't want to take pleasure in someone else's struggle or hardship, but the truth is that there is always someone out there who has it tougher. Yes, I have one son with special needs, but my other son is a gifted writer and student. Not to say he doesn't have struggles, but his are more mundane and manageable. One of my best friends, Amy, has two children with special needs, and I'm a friend to other families who have multiple children with special needs. So when I'm playing my comparison game, why don't I think of them, instead of my friends who have three perfectly healthy children? Lord, help me and help us as we try and try again!

Finding humor in everyday events also helps me step off the comparison treadmill. Once I remember seeing two newbie tennis players who were laughing and having a great time trying to hit the ball. And what were they wearing on their feet? Flip-flops! They were much more fun to watch than the ultra-serious players who sure can kick my bottom in tennis. Another time, I laughed so hard when Luke took the rice milk out of the refrigerator and brought it for help, to his dad, who was sleeping. When Mike failed to respond, Luke plunked himself down on Mike's back and started riding him like a horse! A little rice milk spilled out of the container, but Luke obviously made his point without words. We heard what Luke was saying, loud and clear: "I'm thirsty, and I need some milk RIGHT NOW!"

When I can laugh instead of cry at the funny and often messy things Luke does, it really helps. The comparison game can suck us in and snatch away our joy if we let it. It's so much better to laugh and smile with both my boys than to feel sorry for myself. Last winter we had a big snowfall, but that did nothing to deter Luke from jumping on the trampoline in our yard. He loves the outdoors and he loves to jump! Brandon and I thoroughly enjoyed watching Luke jump as the snow flew all around him. Eventually, Luke made the sign for more, which was his way of saying, "Come jump on the trampoline with me." So we did just that! Without Luke, we would never have experienced the snow jumping. Luke takes us on so many wild adventures. Finding humor in them and living in the moment is so much better than comparing my life to someone else's and coming up short.

I'm slowly learning to focus on the things Luke can do instead of the things he can't. I'm trying to live a life that is full of gratitude for all that our wonderful Father has given me. I'm trying to live a life in which I find humor in day-to-day living and where I think about those who are less fortunate than me more often than comparing myself to those who seem to have everything I want. When I'm able to do this, life on the spectrum can be pretty darn good—both on and off the tennis court.

Discussion Questions:

1. Do you ever find yourself playing the comparison game? If so, how does that make you feel?

2. What are some suggestions that could help you stop comparing your life to others? What are other ways God has shown you to change your thinking?

3. What are some Bible verses that you find helpful when you start to play the comparison game?

Cow Bells and Barricades

KELLI RA ANDERSON

So husbands ought also to love their own wives as their own bodies. He who loves his own wife loves himself; for no one ever hated his own flesh, but nourishes and cherishes it, just as Christ also does the church.

Ephesians 5:28-29, NASB

My first mistake was driving my Honda Fit around the barricade that blocked the residential road through my neighborhood. My second mistake was inadvertently driving into an international bicycle race that had apparently been scheduled that weekend.

Of course, I didn't realize what I'd done until a pace car for the race, (followed by hundreds of speeding cyclists), rounded the empty street corner and came straight toward me. Then it all made sense: the rattling din of cowbells, the frantic arm-waving of the crowds who lined the street, the look of horror on their faces upon my arrival, and their almost universal warning cry, "Pull over!"

Pull over.

How often have I needed to do that? To pull over and take a break from this full-to-the-brim life of middle-aged responsibilities, and autism parenting's relentless demands so full of appointments, dreaded IEPs, millions of daily reminders, and endless to-do lists? I love my children and I love my husband, Adrian, but how many times do I ignore God's prodding to pull over and take care of my marriage and myself so that I can take better care of my family?

It wasn't until I had to write an article about strengthening marriages for couples with special needs children—marriages like my own—that I realized I wasn't exactly practicing what I preached. *Take breaks,* I said. *Go on dates,* I advised. *Hold hands while watching a movie on DVD, sit on the back porch and look up at the stars, and always kiss each other good night,* I insisted. *And above all, at least once a year, get away, just the two of you, no matter what it takes,* I dared to encourage my readers, basing my authority on the words of Paul that speak not just of the sexual health of our marriages, but also of the importance of nourishing and cherishing those we have pledged ourselves to for life (Ephesians 5:28).

I'd told others what to do, but what about my own marriage? I realized how badly Adrian and I needed to heed the barricade God put around our marriage to protect us and take time to replenish a love tank that often teetered on empty. No wonder we felt so weak. We'd been away from our children only once in 17 years after we started our family. Once. For twenty-four hours.

Of course we had our reasons. The state of our finances is the big one, and it's why my husband and I often joke about robbing a bank, or winning the lottery, or coming into an inheritance. We've been joking for years because we have been in debt practically since the day our first child was born, despite many, many plans and schemes and dreams to bob our heads above the financial waters.

You name it, and we've been billed for it: various kinds of therapies, testing, doctors' visits, hospital services, counseling of every shape and size, enough medications to open a fleet of pharmacies, specialty clothing, specialty bedding, a breathing apparatus, special schools, special foods, and pretty much anything and everything we thought might help our two autistic sons and their neurotypical sister cope in the process.

We wonder each time we sit down to view the weekly budget how we will make the numbers fit. It can be so depressing and discouraging, which is why paying bills is not recommended as a precursor to date night.

Sometimes, in our search for a way out of the financial hole, we look back to the day we first pledged to love each other "for richer or for poorer". We wonder if we had just done something differently, if maybe none of this would have happened?

But what can you do when, despite a hard-working husband's good pay, stock markets nosedive and wipe out savings, pension contributions or medical premiums keep rising and pay is frozen and medical care needs overwhelm your income? Looking back over the many ways God has helped us survive, I answer, *Thank you, God. Thank you for helping up make it this far and for the wisdom to do the next thing right.*

The next right thing was to pull over and take care of our strained nerves and starving relationship. Only there was one more barricade. One more thing blocking our willingness to step out in faith: fear that a night or two away would end in a disaster of epic proportions for our family.

Like so many in this transient culture, we don't have extended family nearby to help us lighten the load of special-needs parenting. Realistically, even if they were nearby, their poor health would disqualify them, no matter how much they might want to help with their grandchildren. And we never developed a support system that would allow us the freedom to get away.

Instead, we have a history littered with the debris of interrupted date nights. (One of our favorites is the time a terrified babysitter called us home early because she couldn't find our son. A neighbor finally discovered him hiding under their idling car in his creative effort to win at hide-and-seek.) And we have experienced a season when they were too old for a sitter but not safe enough to be left alone, so we simply shelved date nights altogether.

But one morning over a cup of coffee, God answered that concern, too. He spoke through a dear friend whose greater life experience with teens and disability shed much-needed light on some perspective-changing truth. She told me about a couple who tried for years to find time away together, but every time they tried they were called home early because of issues related to their autistic adult daughter. Until one day, finally, their daughter learned to cope enough that they were able to spend some time away. *Don't give up*, was the take-away lesson. *It will probably fail the first time you try it. And the second. And the third. Sometimes we fail many times before we learn how to get it right.* Adrian and I prayed about it and decided it was time to try.

So my husband got online and booked a weekend away in a nearby state park with cozy cabins we'd enjoyed many years before we had children. Several weeks later, we left our teen sons at home with as much support in place as we could possibly muster (multiple friends to visit them, lists posted for everything imaginable, emergency numbers, premade meals, and lots and lots of prayer).

Turns out, our worst fears did not come true. I am happy to report we only got one phone call, and it wasn't for directions to the hospital. For forty-eight wonderful hours, Adrian and I slept when we wanted, took walks in the woods when we felt like it, and just enjoyed some precious time with each other to experience the peace that comes from doing absolutely nothing.

When we finally got home, we learned some things had not actually gone as we had planned. Judging from the piles of empty wrappers and bags littering the house, we learned our sons preferred to live on Doritos, Cheez-Its, and McDonald's, rather than the meals we'd prepared. But that was so minor. They took their meds. They had gotten along. They even resolved some conflict without involving us!

But alas, no real-life story ever ends happily ever after. We all live in fits and starts. We have since had date nights cut short from sibling fights gone very wrong. There have even been weeks where we've not been able to leave them alone with each other or by themselves. So we've adapted. We've managed to pull over and rest in other ways, like turning off the TV at night and just talking or reading a book together. These little but good things help us keep our marriage tank from red-lighting on empty.

God calls us to take care of our children. He also calls on us to care for our marriages. And in so doing, there are boundaries we must heed and times we must pull over to rest and recharge our relational batteries in any way we can.

Hopefully next time it won't take cowbells and a pace car to make me realize that it's time.

Discussion Questions:

1. Which fear is keeping you from risking growth, either for yourself or for your children?

2. What conversation with God can you have that may challenge you to pull over and do things differently than you previously dared?

3. How can you improve your get-away time with your spouse?

Expectations

KEVIN R. O'BRIEN

For now we see only a reflection as in a mirror; then we shall see face to face.
Now I know in part; then I shall know fully, even as I am fully known.
1 Corinthians 13:12, NIV

Life rarely turns out the way you envision it will when you are
sixteen. I never have been able to settle in my mind whether that
is good or bad. I guess it just is. Perhaps it's a bit of both. My life
is certainly not what I pictured back then. It's like that old Rod
Stewart song rattling around in my brain right now: "I wish that I
knew what I know now when I was younger. . .."

But I digress. Expectations.

We've all got them. They may be more or less conscious.
We may be more or less honest about them, but they're still there.
I have had several sets of expectations for my life over the years. I
can say with the kind of certainty that I am rarely comfortable
with that I did not expect the life that I am now leading. Not at all.

I'm now on the wrong side of forty. Married—to a
Canadian (she's also American now, too). We have three kids: two
boys, one girl. The oldest, Connor, is thirteen. It's hard enough
coming to terms with being over forty. Having a teenager is a
totally mind-blowing experience. I try to be the cool dad. I tell my
oldest that he can dye his hair green, and he looks at me with a

slightly incredulous look and says, "Why would I want to do that?" How am I supposed to stay young with a kid like that?

My youngest made me a believer in a phrase that a college friend once told me several years after we had entered the "real world": "Kevin, my boys are my pride, but my daughters are my joy." There is a deep truth there. A truth I could not fathom until it happened to me. Sierra's my girly girl who's into pink and clothes and power tools and building things with me, who yells "Daddy!" every time I come home. I love it.

And then there's Nathan.

There's so much balled up into that one small sentence. There is love and loss; there is wonder and fear. There is so, so much.

Nathan is twelve. He likes many of the things that his older brother likes. But there is a difference. A difference I never predicted. Never even thought about. Even though, as the oldest of four kids myself, I knew that they would be different.

Nathan has autism.

I love my son more than I can express. I want the best for him. I want him to be happy and loved. I want him to know God and to place him first. And most days, I simply hope that we will get through it all without too many meltdowns, too much opposition, without too much work.

Nathan has higher functions than many who have a diagnosis of autism. He's verbal. He's affectionate (sometimes too affectionate). If you were to see Nathan on the street or in the store, you wouldn't notice that he is different. He looks "normal"—whatever that means.

But Nathan doesn't do abstract thinking. He can't tell you *why* something happened. He can't draw an inference from several facts. He can spell almost everything. He loves to draw and play with Legos. He quotes videos he loves incessantly. He mashes up the things he loves in interesting ways—currently there is a drawing of "The Bird-vengers" on my kitchen table. That would be a mash-up of Angry Birds and The Avengers. (Don't ask. I have no idea. I'm not sure who is who, though there is one bird who appears to be holding Thor's hammer.) Nate is convinced that the best music is from the '80s (I blame his mother), and therefore, "Party Rock" and "Dynamite" are in his "Top 100 songs of the '80s" playlist, never mind that he's about twenty years off (he also knows #37 on his mother's most played list). He is often amused for reasons no one can seem to fathom. And he absolutely loves his cat, Stella.

You never know what Nathan is going to come up with next. It's an adventure. I alternately feel as though I wouldn't trade his quirkiness as an autistic boy for anything and that there is nothing that I wouldn't do to "cure" him so that he could live a normal life.

There's that word again. Normal. It practically shouts our cultural expectations. Our. Mine. I want. I expect. I. I. I.

Maybe I can get past what I want, but what about what my wife wanted for him? What about what he wants? In his mind, he's going to get married (he knows the girl), have six kids, and live in Oswego (Grandma lives there). How do I explain to him that these things probably are not to be?

How do you explain life, love, hope, God to him, or the fact that he probably cannot live on his own? There are a hundred thoughts in my mind right now of what he can't do, what he will never experience.

And I *hate* it.

My wife tries to tell our kids not to use that word. But sometimes it's appropriate. This is one of those times.

My faith is central to who I am. It is not something tacked on, an appendage to make me feel better. I do not have "my best life now" and still I believe. I believe more deeply today, in and through Nathan's life, than I did when I was sixteen.

But.

How do you help a twelve-year-old boy who cannot think abstractly understand God?

How do you explain the need for redemption to a child who hears at church that he is supposed to be like Jesus who is perfect and is then totally discombobulated when someone tells him that he himself is not perfect and will not be—and that's okay? How do I as a father, an elder, a minister, reach into his life and convey the deep truths of faith to him?

After all, he is teaching me.

God, I found out recently, lives in Geneva, Switzerland, along with Francis A. Schaeffer. This was news to me, but it dawned on me that Nathan sat in on the Sunday School class I taught using Schaeffer's *How Then Shall We Live* series. Apparently he was paying more attention than I thought, even if he did get some of the details wrong. The nearest I can figure, Nate connected Schaeffer's discussions about God on location in Geneva and decided both lived there. It's humorous, but it also illustrates the difficulty of having a child who takes things so literally. I asked Nate some follow-up questions to figure out the connections he was making. Mostly I asked questions about God. In Nathan's mind, of course, God has a body. He's a person, isn't he? People have bodies. It's simply the way that it works.

In the grand scheme of things, helping Nathan understand that God doesn't have a body is a fairly small thing. But it's only the tip of the iceberg. One recent Sunday was interesting. There was an impromptu baptismal service after the worship service was done. Nathan wanted to be baptized, but not for the right reasons. He didn't really understand what it was all about. He wanted people to clap for him. So I set about trying to explain it—to a kid who really doesn't get the concept of salvation to begin with.

And so I have gone looking for resources. What I have found so far is this. Few churches have any idea what to do with kids like Nathan. Special needs children and their families rarely go to church. It's difficult. It requires extra effort. It's exhausting. And if you are lucky enough to find a church that does have something, it's usually a buddy (which is fantastic), who isn't really sure what to do (not so great, but that can be dealt with). When they're younger, and if they are like Nathan, they can probably stay in regular classes. But they won't be doing what everyone else is doing. They won't be integrated. Not really. And then junior high hits. And suddenly, even the churches that have created sensory rooms and buddies and programs for parents to get out once a month don't know what to do.

And then there are the expectations. Families want their kids to be included in the wider programs, to be a part of those who would be their peers. Often it's just not realistic. I know this, and I'm the dad. I still want Nate to form real relationships. To grow. To become.

Church should be the first place where this can happen. But we simply do not know what to do or how to act.

So here I am. Tired of waiting for someone to fix it. Tired of expectations that have been sacrificed on the altar of expedience and ignorance. Tired of letting autism happen to my family, to my son.

In the Old Testament, Nathan was a prophet. We don't know much about him, other than the fact that he had the audacity to call the king on the carpet. My Nathan has been a prophet in my own life. One who has the unwitting audacity to demand that I answer the question, "What are you going to do about me? What are you going to do about the fact that the Church doesn't know what to do with me, how to teach me, how to show me Jesus?" The thing is, he doesn't even know that he's asking.

I don't have all of the answers. Don't even know all of the right questions, I'm sure. But the thing about faith is that it isn't sight.

Discussion Questions:

1. How have you had to adjust your expectations for your life or your child's life?

2. How has living with someone on the spectrum affected your faith? Do you feel it more keenly now than before, or have you become distanced? Why is that?

3. How can you help your church to see the needs of children on the spectrum through Jesus' eyes?

Gambling on God's Grace

KATHLEEN DEYER BOLDUC

When Jacob awoke from his sleep, he thought, "Surely the Lord is in this place, and I was not aware of it." He was afraid and said, "How awesome is this place! This is none other than the house of God; this is the gate of heaven."

Genesis 28:16-17, NIV

Theologian Søren Kierkegaard once wrote, "Life can only be understood backwards; but it must be lived forwards." His words speak directly to my heart as Joel's mom. Joel is a handsome twenty-nine-year-old man, who has autism and moderate intellectual disabilities. God meets me daily on this journey of motherhood, enabling me to let go of future fears and past regrets, empowering me to lean fully into today even as I walk into the future. God has given me gifts of wisdom and discernment, as I look back and remember God's faithful presence every step of the way.

I had a light-bulb moment fifteen years ago as I sat in the waiting room of Joel's play therapist. I was struggling with feelings of self-pity, exhaustion, and guilt. It was summer time, and I was angry that my family couldn't take the fun vacations our friends' families were taking. Only the beach for us, familiar and undemanding. But as I zoned out, staring at a Monet poster on the wall, I stepped out of time and stood on the bridge in Monet's

25

garden. I suddenly knew I wanted to change the lens through which I viewed our life with autism. I wrote a poem about it, entitled "Waiting Rooms." The last stanzas of that poem read:

> I wonder
> Can I carve a garden
> from the weedy turf of life
> plant colors of my choosing
> in arrangements pleasing to my eye
> weed out thistles
> of resentment and fear
> replace them with flowers
> of joy and contentment?
> Suspended between past and future
> in this waiting room
> today
> I weave a garden plan of beauty
> while I wait
> for my son (From *Autism & Alleluias*, Judson Press, 2010)

When I wrote this poem, life was hard. Daily meltdowns—too many to count. Sleepless nights—again, too many to count. Too many doctors. Too many people sitting around the table during too many IEP meetings. Too many family times disrupted by behaviors.

But in that waiting room I heard God calling me to look for the blessings in the midst of too-muchness and too-manyness—to look for His presence right here, right now, in the realm of the just-right.

And so I began to search for and meditate on those places where God's grace glimmered on a day-by-day basis. A good book at bedtime. Chasing rainbows in the car with Joel. One-on-one time with Matt and Justin while Joel hung out with Dad. The squish of sand between my toes and the caress of a soft sea breeze on those yearly beach vacations.

We played it safe, up until Joel's twenty-eighth year, sticking with beach vacations, branching out to a cabin in the mountains on occasion. Always with additional help accompanying us so that Wally and I could have a bit of "couple time," and everyone could return home refreshed and restored.

But this year we gambled on God's grace. We took Joel, without additional staff, on a vacation to Long Island, New York, to visit with our ministry partners from Bridge for Peace (a worldwide healing ministry). The six-day trip included a plane flight from Cincinnati to La Guardia, a taxi ride to Jamaica Station to catch the Long Island Railroad, an hour-long train ride to Ronconcomo Station halfway out the Island, and another forty-minute car ride from there to our friends' house.

A lot for a guy with sensory issues to handle, but handle it he did, with aplomb. (Great restraint shown under even the most trying circumstances.) And there were more than a few trying circumstances: a four-hour delay in the Cincinnati airport, putting us in New York at rush hour; navigating LaGuardia Airport where the entire population of New York seemed to be converging; a crazy taxi ride through traffic; finding our way to the ticket counter through a bustling Jamaica Train Station, and two minutes, from the moment we bought our train tickets, to find and board our train. Yikes! Not an easy feat for anyone after a full day of travel, much less someone who hates crowds and has never before wheeled his own suitcase!

Once settled in at our friends' house, Joel slept in a strange bed, met many new people, sat through a two-hour prayer meeting, and was asked to pray for people he didn't know (Joel is on our prayer team at home, so he's used to hands-on prayer, but generally with people he knows).

Gambling on God's grace isn't really a gamble. It's a sure bet. Mixed in with the trying circumstances were many unforgettable vacation moments: a four hour "Praise Cruise" with Bridge for Peace on Long Island's Great South Bay (where Joel's exuberant worship lit up his corner of the boat, blessing everyone who watched him), long walks on the beach, a trip to the aquarium, leisurely meals around the table with dear friends (after which Joel retired to the couch with his iPad—*thank you, Lord!*), a concert on the beach, and a relaxing day at a friend's pool.

Life can only be understood backwards; but it must be lived forwards.

God encourages me to choose life every single day, empowering me to move forward, living life—just as Joel lived his vacation—with aplomb (another definition for this wonderful word is "grace under pressure").

This is what I know to be true: I have a daily choice to look at life with autism through the lens of God's blessings or through the lens of "woe is me." The gift of watching Joel navigate trains, planes, and automobiles with the assurance of a seasoned traveler would never have happened if I did not lean into God's promise that He is the same yesterday, today, and tomorrow, and that He has been, is, and will be with us every step of the journey.

I praise God for Joel's vacation this year. So many stones of remembrance to pick up and revisit when life gets hard again—as it will, without a doubt. So many reasons to lean into today, knowing I'm walking in God's presence. In the words of the song "In God's Presence" (by our good friend Kevin McKernan): "In

God's presence / Wisdom unsearchable / Riches incomparable / Grace inexhaustible."

Discussion Questions:

1. When have you experienced God's inexhaustible grace in the past week? The past month? The past year?

2. Take some time today to revisit your "ebenezers," or stones of remembrance—those places where God has met you along the journey (I Samuel 7:12). Those places where you suddenly realized, as Jacob did, that "Surely the LORD is in this place, and I was not aware of it." (Genesis 28:16, NIV)

The Threshold of Gratitude

MICHELE BOVELL

*Being strengthened with all power, according to his glorious might, for all
endurance and patience with joy; giving thanks to the Father, who has
qualified you to share in the inheritance of the saints in light. He has delivered
us from the domain of darkness and transferred us to the kingdom of his
beloved Son, in whom we have redemption, the forgiveness of sins.*
                                                    Colossians 1:11-14, ESV

We were fellow black mothers of children on the spectrum—
educated, well-informed, and ambitious in our shared goal to help
our children achieve their greatest potential, if not lick autism
altogether. We had all met at an Atlanta conference on autism, and
one among us had taken on the task of gathering contact
information and arranging a get-together. We met every few weeks
over the course of a year. It was good to talk—good to dress up,
get out of the house, and share a meal and a glass of wine. It was
especially good to feel as though someone was listening and could
truly empathize. While my boys were newly diagnosed, these ladies
were seasoned advocates for their children. We spoke of the latest
therapies and research, of the best schools and practitioners, and
of our shared quest to access disability resources and support. As
we got closer and freer with each other, someone eventually
broached the subject of her failing marriage. With several of the
women divorced or otherwise single parenting, that topic easily
aroused emotions. Conversations moved away from proactive

steps on behalf of our children and began to take on an astringent undertone of frustration—with parents, partners, support persons, children.

We all get there at some point. The finality of the diagnosis and the way autism pervades our lives as parents and caregivers can leave us in a constant battle against despondency and hopelessness. But what I have come to learn and live is that a Gospel-informed worldview provides a foundation of hope, which over and over pulls us up from melancholy and redirects our thoughts to greater truths than the reality that immediately confronts us. Thanksgiving overrides the inclination to despair.

I have five sons. Like many new mothers, I began parenting with high hopes for my children. When my firstborn was young, I kept track of developmental milestones and was quick to report his achievements to all who would hear. When the boys on the spectrum arrived, the boasting ended. Autism changed the criteria for successful parenting. Outcomes were unpredictable, and praise and approval from my peers were soon replaced by pity and at least perceived judgment. Parenting became a private affair, with progress largely missed by those outside the inner circle of immediate family, teachers, and therapists. When progress is slow and comes in small events, one must lower the threshold of gratitude, or else bitterness and disillusionment creep in. It takes a habit of rejoicing in all things to stave off melancholy, and it takes divine aid to rejoice when we are at the end of ourselves.

In the early years, it was much easier. The children were beautiful, and their delays kept them in a sweet state of innocence for a long time—no willfulness, no back talk, no defiance. A small team of special educators, therapists, and advocates were all invested in their success. There were frustrations, but I carried in my heart the conviction that all would be OK. Ethan, my eldest, was making remarkable progress, and I received praise for my good work with the boys. Autism also gave me a narrative—a story to tell. If I no longer fit in the regular mom's club, there was always the one for martyrs. There was somewhat of a payoff to being the long-suffering mother of two with special needs, and all that research and conference attending had armed me with knowledge that made for good conversation.

There were good and tangible reasons to celebrate and be thankful: My marriage had not only survived but had thrived as we banded together to raise our boys and attack autism. (We didn't have the luxury of fighting.) Choosing to homeschool, after special needs preschool, eliminated the common frustration of negotiating with the public school for services. Georgia had no shortage of private therapists ready to accept the state's disability funding. We had enough of what we needed, and so we rejoiced and thanked God openly; but thanksgiving would become more challenging in the years that followed.

Theologian A. W. Tozer said something to the effect that it takes a different level of faith to thank God for blessings unrealized than it does for those experienced in the past or currently enjoyed. Thanksgiving does not come as easily to us in the lean years, but the lean years are training years, and God-directed gratitude is what sustains us in them. With the birth of our fourth and fifth sons, my family and I began a descent into isolation and away from familiar supports. Caring for an infant and toddler again meant less social interaction and mobility. The boys were discharged from therapies, and so we lost that regular feedback and assistance from professionals. Then, when our fifth child was a toddler, our family made an ill-advised move to a rural Midwestern town to work with an organization. The partnership quickly failed, leaving us alone and without friends and family, and unable to locate a single support group or autism specialist. Most significant, we were without the consistent fellowship of a community of believers. This season of trial certainly weakened our spirits and we were tempted to despair, yet it became one of the most meaningful experiences of our lives. We cried out for relief, but it did not come as we expected. Instead, the Lord redirected our attention to the greater gift in his Son.

Recently, I read a quote by author, Roger Hershey that said, "If we don't have a good eternal perspective, we'll become captivated by the temporary...." That was at the heart of where my husband and I were a little over a decade ago. We were longtime Christians, convinced of the Gospel, and committed to righteous living, but whether it was ministry opportunity, job, or aid for our children, what we largely focused on and where we sought joy and fulfillment were here, right now, in what we could see. This made for a shaky hope.

Autism has a way of eclipsing everything else in our lives. It can become the sole determiner of peace and well-being, particularly when one is isolated from the people who can help bring perspective. But there in the cornfields, through Christian books, messages on CD, and sermons found online, the Lord began to renew our minds by returning us to the basics of the Gospel message—truth independent of our subjective experiences: "He has delivered us from the domain of darkness and transferred us to the kingdom of his beloved Son, in whom we have redemption, the forgiveness of sins." Apprehension of that truth—that regardless of what we interpret as gloom in this life, we have been saved from a far greater darkness, and that we stand in Light that no disability or hardship can eclipse, truly grasping the sacrifice of the Son, and understanding our helplessness to offer anything of merit in our own salvation— have been the pathway out of fickle hope and into solid joys. It has also been the key to God-directed gratitude—the recognition that "Every good gift and every perfect gift is from above, coming down from the Father of lights..." (James 1:17, ESV).

As believers, we wait to fully inherit the benefits of our adoption in Christ, but our Father gives us gifts now, and we can rejoice in them as reminders of our true position in Christ. Lowering the threshold of gratitude is not about settling for less, but about finding more with which to be thankful.

Discussion Questions:

1. Are your hopes and joys placed in things temporal or eternal?

2. Despite the daily pressures of life with a loved one on the spectrum, can you identify God-given gifts and grace for which to give thanks?

3. Are there godly people in your life, or resources such as sermons, blogs, and books that can help you to gain God's perspective and assist you to develop a habit of thanksgiving?

The Other Side to Suffering

MICHAEL ABBS

Dear friends, do not be surprised at the painful trial you are suffering, as though something strange were happening to you.

1 Peter 4:12, NIV

Why is this verse so difficult to remember? Why am I still surprised or annoyed when the suffering comes? I suppose there are no easy answers, and I know I am not the only one who asks these questions.

In one sense, this has been a rough year for me. I have been sick much of the time. Our new roof is taking in a large amount of water, and there is some still-unknown damage to be repaired. The weather has been relentlessly cold and snowy, even for the Midwest. Luke, my nine-year-old son who has autism, has been sick much of the year, too. This, coupled with the normal struggles related to autism, has made it especially rough on all of us.

But in another sense, it has also been a great year so far, and it all has to do with how I see God working in me. I have been able to see these struggles, not as tragedies, but rather as opportunities to become more of who God wants me to be, to get closer to Him, and to know His perfect peace and joy.

As is often the case when it comes to my spiritual growth, it seems to have much more to do with God working through the

Spirit than any special effort on my part. God seems to use illness or other difficulties in my life to help me submit and lean on Him. When I feel bad physically, Jesus is close and points out what is important in life. He certainly does not show me things like what other people think of me, or money, or material possessions. But, rather, what is more important is eternal realities, being close to God and sharing Him with others.

God is teaching me more about this all the time. There are specific times of hardship that I can point to in the last twenty years where this has definitely been the case. These are moments that have helped me get to the point where I can more easily embrace, though not necessarily enjoy, hardships.

In 1995 I became a police officer—my dream career for as long as I can remember. I found the demands of learning and performing the job to be high. The stress climbed steadily. For a number of months, during field training, all actions and interactions of the recruit are observed, scrutinized, and rated. It is necessary and important. Some don't make it through this portion of the training process, and I certainly didn't want to join that category. Officers turn to different things for strength and stress relief—some comforts are destructive in the long run. For me, though, this became an opportunity for growth in my relationship with God. I was growing closer to God, and discovering how to lean on Him and experience more inner strength and peace.

The next period of major growth for me occurred a few years later. My wife Deb became pregnant and our first son, Brandon, was born in 1999. Deb immediately became very sick. She had to stay in the hospital for an extended time. In the midst of that storm God was there, for her and for me. I remember feeling close with the heavenly Father in a way I had not experienced before. On the outside, there was more uncertainty, stress, and responsibility than I had ever faced. I was still new in my police career, and it was going well. I was already a field-training officer, which means I was training and rating others instead of being trained and rated. And I was new to the department SWAT team. I was not well-positioned to take a period of extended time off, and I didn't want to seem unreliable. I have always had a real sense of duty to be there every day for the job, knowing that a sick day could mean my fellow officers could be left short-handed and possibly at risk, as a result.

Despite the job pressures, my bigger concern was for Deb and baby Brandon. Could I take care of him well enough by myself? Would Deb be healthy, happy, and here for us? Peace and God's strength met this worry, this trial, in a real way for me. A new knowledge of God's sovereignty and His love for me was clear for me to see and feel. God was working as I submitted to Him. I knew I was being molded into someone who could handle these and other trials.

I think about how this idea of hardships and growth works with our son, Luke, too. When Luke was born, after a difficult and dangerous delivery, he came home with us and folded nicely into our family, which by this time included our Pomeranian, Chewie. I was the department's firearms range master and training coordinator, and I was preparing for a promotion to sergeant. Despite the difficult delivery, Deb had a much better pregnancy and was enjoying little Luke.

Luke started growing up without noticeable problems. After a couple of years he was talking some, but there were signs that something may not be right. His speech developed slowly, and he had some strange rocking and flapping movements developing. After some tests, we received the autism diagnosis.

I don't remember ever being floored or devastated by it. I have always been an optimist, and this tendency has carried into my feelings about his progress and future. But more than that was a God-given inner peace. In His Word, we see that God has always been there for His children and has promised that He always would be. In my life, God has always come through for me, too. It was clear to me that this diagnosis, and the unknown future that accompanied it, was not going to be too much to handle for any of us. God was going to come through again. To me, that didn't mean Luke would be physically healed, though I have always been open to that possibility. Rather, it meant God would give us the strength, wisdom, and peace to survive and thrive. He was going to use this to impact us and others.

Over time, I have found from discussions with friends and family that women and men can actually respond differently to a special needs diagnosis in their children, which can make it hard to relate to each other in ways we need. Although my experience alone doesn't qualify as any scientific study, it does seem to me that men are typically more able than women to relate to and understand my response to my son's diagnosis. Looking at my marriage to my wife, Deb, as my closest example, it seems evidence of another way God has made us different but complimentary. Without her, I'm sure I would not have been as proactive in getting Luke the diagnosis and help he has needed. Without me, Deb admits she would have panicked even more about the diagnosis and setbacks related to Luke's special needs.

In spite of all this, God has plans for Luke. Without Luke saying a word, it seems that one of God's plans for Luke is to use him to move others toward a career focused on those with special needs or to help them stay the course. One of his former therapists, in fact, has cited Luke as the reason she has gone into full time special needs education. Prior to working with Luke, another of his therapists, Jason, wasn't sure he wanted to continue working in social services. Autism Home Support Services told him about a boy who needed his help (Luke), and he decided to at least come meet Luke and our family. He figured if it didn't seem right, he wouldn't commit to working with Luke. After the first meeting Jason's wife told him that she hadn't heard him talk so passionately about helping someone in a long time. "Even though my wife believed, I was still hesitant to believe that this was where I belonged and what I am basically hard-wired to do. But it didn't take long after that, simply because Luke made me believe," explains Jason. Currently Jason works full-time as a dean at a school for children with behavioral challenges.

While it is not always easy to give the extra care that he needs, it is right—right where God wants him to be and right where He wants us to be. So Luke's autism is more than a hardship. It is a blessing on many levels and another opportunity to grow stronger and closer to our Lord and Savior, Jesus Christ.

Which brings me back to the start of this year. I think that these past trials and hardships have brought me to the point where, at least sometimes, I can look at difficult circumstances, and like James said, I can "consider it pure joy, my brothers and sisters, whenever you face trials of many kinds, because you know that the testing of your faith produces perseverance." (James 1:2-3, NIV) I can remind myself that the difficult times can be a benefit to me and an opportunity to grow more into the person God wants me to be.

Discussion Questions:

1. When you think of a difficult time in your life, what do you think God was trying to teach you? How did you grow?

2. What can you do when struggles come again?

3. Do you think there may be truth to the idea that men and women may deal with difficulties, especially when it comes to their children on the spectrum, differently? What could this mean for us as Christian parents?

Never Stop Praying

KELLI RA ANDERSON

Pray continually, give thanks in all circumstances; for this is God's will for you in Christ Jesus.

1 Thessalonians 5:17-18, NIV

As Miley and I turned the corner on our morning dog walk, I saw the most beautiful sight. My eighteen-year-old son, dressed in his short-sleeved work shirt, was standing at the street corner, waving an eager goodbye as he stepped onto the short bus. "I did it!" he cried out before the bus doors closed behind him and drove him away to begin his day. I waved in return, a frosty cloud of breath exhaled in relief.

Never mind that he hadn't remembered his hoodie to keep warm. Never mind that he left the signed letter he was supposed to take with him to his counselor on the kitchen counter. There, on that same counter, were the medication bottles he remembered to remove from their shelf and a telltale glass of partially finished water. And there, on the street corner, had been the answer to my morning's fervent prayers that he would take that one big step out the door, that one giant leap toward independence.

He had gotten on the bus without my help.

Earlier this morning I turned to 1 Thessalonians 5:17, "Never stop praying" (NLT) and then to Proverbs 3:6 that underscored Paul's message with an emphatic, "Seek his will in all you do and he will show you which path to take" (NLT).

God knew what I needed. I needed to stop looking at the clock, watching the minutes tick away while my son continued to stay in his bed, even as his bus was on its way to pick him up for his transition program at 8:05 a.m. God knew I needed to stop being his human alarm clock and that I needed to let him fail, if necessary (as he had the week before). And God knew I needed to let him see that he could also succeed.

I looked at the clock. It read 7:53 and my heart began to pound in spite of my good intentions to trust. "Please, God, oh, please get him out of bed. Let him succeed. Please show him that he can do this." I looked at the clock again and then at God's words, "Seek his will . . . he will show you which path to take." I needed to leave the house, and I needed to keep praying.

I reached for my dog's leash, snapped it onto Miley's collar, and opened the front door of our house. "Mom?" came my son's fearful voice from his bedroom. "I need your help!"

"No, you don't," I called back with a confidence I didn't feel. "You know what to do and I have to take Miley for a walk." Then I added, "Have a great day at work, okay? See you this afternoon!" and I closed the door behind me.

For the next 7 minutes, I walked around our block. I prayed and I tried to surrender. What if he missed the bus again? What if I'd made the wrong decision? I prayed some more and surrendered again. Then, the words of a hymn I hadn't heard in years came into my mind. "Be still my soul, the Lord is on your side . . . leave to your God to order and provide."

I pushed back at my fears. God is the one to order and to provide. It was time to pray and let Him be the one John is learning to rely on, not me. Even if it means that he learns the hard way.

When I turned the corner and saw my son standing there, dressed and ready for work, waiting for the bus, all I could breathe out was a repetitious line of thank yous to God for this one moment of progress.

Never stop praying.

I know that this doesn't mean John is cured or that he will never miss his bus again. I know God doesn't work like that. (Or else I am seriously turning my prayers to urgent issues like not being able to find my keys. Or my shoes. Or the reason I find myself going into rooms and not remembering why.)

But I also know that God is at work and He is working hard to direct our paths. Daily prayer--constant prayer--is the hand-holding I need to remind me He knows what He's doing and I can trust Him to take the lead.

Never stop praying.

This isn't the first time I have had to learn this lesson. It's not even the hundredth time. In the world of special needs parenting, we find ourselves more often than most, having to rely on prayer multiple times a day. But in Thessalonians, Paul didn't just tell his beloved brothers and sisters in Christ to pray. Immediately following that instruction, he added, "Be thankful in all circumstances . . . hold on to what is good" (I Thessalonians 5:18,21, NLT). Prayer for our needs and thankfulness for His mercies are two sides of the same coin.

I have kept a journal since I was twelve years old. It's sort of a life-long survival skill that helps to keep me sane, but for anyone who might read them one day, the journals may also convince them writing in my journal plus Prozac might have been a better recipe for success. Hindsight is truly 20/20.

But my journal from ten years ago contains something that has since become an essential practice; I began a daily observance of something that gives me joy.

These entries weren't just niceties. They were necessities when I found myself clinically depressed and facing the possibility of our third child's diagnosis with autism. That time, one of our darkest, also became a turning point in my relationship with God. Overrun with therapies, doctors' bills, teachers' calls for help, nightly chaos at home, and a medicine cabinet that rivaled the shelves of Walgreens, I came to the end of what I could do in my own strength.

I turned to God, and in tears and despair I waved the white flag of surrender and hopelessness. What He showed me in return was that I needed Him, and lots of Him, just one day at a time. I wasn't going to get the answers I needed all at once. There was no magic pill and no cure-all therapy or miracle diet. There was no quick fix or maybe not even a slow one. My only hope was to see my life through His eyes, and the first thing He asked me to do was to be thankful for whatever I could find, no matter how small.

In the dark basement family room the afternoon He first presented this idea to me, it didn't seem like I could find a single flicker of light to be grateful for. But I sat down to my journal, and I obediently wrote the date on the page and paused, thinking, thinking, thinking. And then I wrote one thing. A ridiculously small thing. And then another.

Each day, no matter how impossible things seemed, I began to see what God could see and I began to have hope, even in the middle of toilet training gone wild and sleep disorders run amok. One day, I was only able to write that I was grateful for my youngest son David's rodent, a dwarf Siberian hamster, Ralphie, that had made me smile when David would present him each morning to me like a treasured gift, curled up in the palm of his little hand. Another day it was only that my daughter smiled. I was learning to hold onto the good.

Today may things are so much things better. But we face new challenges as every family does, including one that only last night had two of us sitting on the floor of our bathroom in tears. But there are victories, too.

This morning I wrote that my oldest son got on the bus without help. But I think I was wrong. He did have help. He had God's help. And God is helping me. Through the prayers I now sprinkle with thanksgiving, I am experiencing gratitude for what may seem like small victories to others, but to me they seem worthy of a ticker-tape parade. God knows what we need. We need Him, and He is eager to be found. Never stop praying.

Discussion Questions:

1. What victories, no matter how small, are you able to see and celebrate and give thanks for today?

2. What issues in your life today are you tackling in your own strength that you need to stop and first lay down at God's feet in prayer?

3. If prayer is not a regular part of your day, where can you make a place, no matter how small or for how brief a time, one where you can pour your heart out to God?

4. Paul ends his letter in 1 Thessalonians 5:28 (NLT) with this sentence: "May the grace of our Lord Jesus Christ be with you." Grace means God's blessing is ours even when the world may look, or see, otherwise. God's blessing is ours even when we look at our failings as parents, and it seems otherwise. His grace is with us. Where is His blessing in your life?

It Takes a Village . . . or Two or Three

DEBORAH ABBS

Carry each other's burdens, and in this way you will fulfill the law of Christ.
Galatians 6:2, NIV

The saying goes that "It takes a village to raise a child." Anyone caring for a person on the autism spectrum knows that is simply *not* true. Why? Because it doesn't take just one. Two, three, or maybe even four villages are needed to do the job.

Here's the other reality that really scares me and causes me to plead with God for help when I dwell on it too much: It's not just a phase.

You know how the thought "It's just a phase" or "This is temporary" gets you through the day when you have a newborn who keeps you up all night? What happens when your child or teen or adult is up at night with no end in sight?

A downright messy example is potty training. Potty training my "typical" son, Brandon, was work, but I knew it was temporary. After a short time, he had it down and didn't have any more bathroom accidents. However, with Luke, my nine-year-old son who has autism, we literally have been in potty training mode for *years*. And there's no way to know when he will be accident free. For a while, Luke wore underwear all day at school and had almost no accidents (his teachers take him to the restroom regularly throughout the day), which was fantastic and cut down

49

on the cost of pull-ups. Recently, he regressed, and we aren't sure why. And this is just *one* struggle we face.

Luke is a smart, affectionate boy who needs constant supervision. Or as constant as we can provide until we are exhausted. At home we can be less vigilant assuming he's indoors. If he makes a mess or is too rough on something, it's just our stuff. But there is no telling what mischief he will get into. He loves water and takes multiple baths a day. We lock the doors to the bathrooms with bathtubs. Where do I find him when we accidentally leave one open? Fully dressed in a tub full of water! After finding him getting into some sort of mischief, my husband or I are often found muttering, "It's a good thing you're cute, otherwise I don't know what I'd do with you, Luke!" or "Ah! The room has been Luked!"

The bathroom isn't the only room on lockdown. The kitchen is too. The refrigerator, all the cabinets, and especially the cabinet underneath our kitchen sink where the cleaning supplies are kept—you get the picture, I'm sure.

Luke absolutely loves the outdoors. Thankfully, we have a tall fence around the backyard so he can enjoy being outside without escaping. Except for when the fence gate falls over, which I usually don't realize until he's gone! Or the time we forgot to close the front door when a handyman was over, and Luke took off. We were so thankful when our neighbor found him a block away at the park safe and sound; after all, he had to cross two streets to get there and does not understand the danger of getting run over. Those minutes he went missing took years off my life here on earth.

When we go to other people's homes, we need to make sure we don't lose him, things don't get wrecked, and hope he doesn't melt down (see more on this in the chapter, "Parties Ain't No Fun Anymore"). It's exhausting just writing all this down! Luke can even make my normally unflappable husband, who as a police officer has chased down burglars and armed assailants, say uncle.

But before I make anyone else curl up in a ball and hide in the corner, here comes the good news. The villages of people who help us in all of this are the biggest blessing. We probably never would have met so many wonderful friends if not for our precious special needs son. These friends include his Applied Behavioral Analysis (ABA) therapists provided by Autism Home Support Services, teachers, aids, social workers, friends made at Joni and Friends family retreat, volunteers at church and Luke's bus driver. We have so many helping hands!

I seriously do not know where we'd be without these folks and the safety net they provide. Some are like extended family to us now, and they just love Luke. So many folks have gone above and beyond their given jobs to help us solve problems. Lizz, one of Luke's former home ABA therapists, is also a great handyman (or in this case a handywoman). Before she came up with a solution to our bathtub troubles, I would constantly have to run up and down the stairs of our two-story house while Luke was in the tub. I'd tell him, "No more water. The tub is full." The next thing I knew, he'd have the faucet on again, adding water to the already full bathtub. Up and down and all around I'd go. Lizz made this wooden box with a door on the front that locks and installed it over the faucet so Luke can't get to it. That one small thing has helped so much!

The only reason my husband, Mike, and I are able to sit together and worship at our church on Sunday mornings is because the church provides a special needs room for Luke and others who need it. He is just too active to sit in the service, and the crowd of people and loud noises can overwhelm him. What a gift and a blessing that not all special needs families have.

People give so much of themselves and their skills to us, but I also know that Luke has touched many lives and taught others so much. First and foremost, he has opened my eyes and taught me so much about how just because you can't talk doesn't mean you're not smart; and how a smile and a hug can communicate love, so much so that words aren't needed. (Although, I still pray all the time that he will get some of his words back!) And Lizz went back to school to get her master's degree in early childhood education in large part because of Luke, and is now teaching full-time.

I'm ashamed to admit the misconceptions I had about those with special needs before Luke was diagnosed with autism. I'm even more ashamed this whole people group wasn't even on my radar at all. The few times I did think about them, I only had preconceived notions that I later discovered were just plain wrong. Before having Luke, I remember seeing a mom holding a baby with Down Syndrome and thinking, "Oh, how sad for her."

Now, I know; shame on me. Because of Luke, my, how I understand! My world has changed, and I see how special that baby is and wonder what wonderful lessons she will teach her mom and others.

That might be the biggest blessing from all of this right there: God has been able to work in my heart and mind to make me notice and love those with special needs and in the process make me more into the person He wants me to be. After all, of the numerous miracles Jesus did that are recorded in the Gospels, many were for someone with a special need—those that were blind, mute, paralyzed. In His day, society overlooked and shunned these people—like many societies still do today. But Jesus did not ignore or shun them; instead He reached out in love.

Thank you, Lord, for sending me Luke to help change my ways that needed to be changed. Thank you for all the people who have, are, and will make up the villages to help raise and care for Luke. I sure don't know how we'd do it without them.

Discussion Questions:

1. Do you find that you need many villages—or a very large one at least—to help you care for your loved one with autism? If so, how has this need for help been met?

2. How do you feel about needing to ask for help?

3. Has God changed your attitude about those with special needs, through your own special needs child? If so, how?

Why versus What

KEVIN O'BRIEN

I waited patiently for the Lord to help me,
and he turned to me and heard my cry.
He lifted me out of the pit of despair,
out of the mud and the mire.
He set my feet on solid ground
and steadied me as I walked along.
He has given me a new song to sing,
a hymn of praise to our God.
Many will see what he has done and be amazed.
They will put their trust in the LORD.

Psalm 40:1-3, NLT

When Nathan was younger, he went to a school with random
sections of green tiles on the hall floors. Sometimes only a few,
other times in great swaths of green. At some point Nate decided
he could not walk on the green tiles. So he had his class taking the
long way around or would get piggyback rides from teachers or
paraprofessionals. I am not making this up or exaggerating in the
least. One time, Nate wasn't paying attention and walked through
a section of green tiles while his class was going to the library. No
one is quite sure what distracted him or when he realized what he
had done. The teacher got to the library with the class and realized
that Nate wasn't there. She retraced her steps, and sure enough,
there was Nate standing all alone on the brown tiles surrounded

by a sea of green. He had realized what he had done and was not going anywhere.

Parents of autistic kids get to tell the best stories.

That one is mildly amusing; many are not. It is only when we get enough distance from the event to blunt the embarrassment or fear that we can see them as great stories. We've all been there. We will be again. The story of Nathan and the green tiles is a fairly mild one, not embarrassing in the least, but it was frustrating. There was no reason that we could think of, no logic that I could discern in which tiles (why green?) or why.

Frustration is the feeling that hits me most. Why is he doing this? Frustration that I can't get through. Frustration that I can't make it better, that I can't fix it.

I grew up in an intensely practical household. My father can and does fix everything. My dad and grandfather built my parents' house. They still live in it. My mother laid flagstone on the front of the house when she was four or five months pregnant with me. I grew up holding lights under cars and holding boards in place as things were being built. There didn't seem to be anything my dad couldn't fix, which was a good thing because stuff always seemed to be breaking.

My dad and I are not alike in many ways, but enough of his fix-it gene has rubbed off on me that I can hold my own in a lot of areas. Not like him, but enough. Plus, I'm a stereotypical guy. I want to fix things. Sue me.

I can't fix this. I can't make my son better. Can't fix my wife's hurt. Can't fix my own.

What do you do when you are faced with the reality that you cannot fix something? That you cannot set a grievous wrong to right? I have a hard time getting my head around it, to be perfectly honest.

My father isn't a teacher; he's a doer. I am by nature a student; I want to think about it. My dad knows how it works. I want to know why. Growing up, I compensated by watching and learning how to break things down into component parts. I would want to figure out the rationale and my dad would say, "I don't want to philosophize about it. I want to get it done." I love philosophy. Maybe that's why I wanted to be a writer when I grew up and did not go to work for Caterpillar like my grandfather, father, and brother.

Here's the thing: As much as I want it, Nate can't give me a why. He can't explain it. And he gives few clues to figure it out. And that is perhaps the hardest part. I want to know why in all kinds of areas because it tells me what to do next. It tells me *if* I should do the next thing. It's how I get to the point where I can fix things. My dad gets in there to get things done. I wonder if I should. I am sure that there are lots of things I haven't done because I have spent far too long wondering why. I should have just jumped in.

Nate jumps in. He does. He manipulates his environment to follow his fancy. And I do mean manipulates in every sense of the word. Sometimes that just means he gets things to work the best way that he can. Sometimes it means he's manipulative in that oh-so-devious sort of way—sidling up to Grandma with a hug and a smooch and an "I love you, Grandma." You just know that he is going to present a request that is oh-so-reasonable in about 2.3 seconds. He knows how to push the right buttons. Sometimes it's comical. Other times, not so much.

Why is rarely an issue for Nate.

"Why are you upset, Nate?"

"Because I'm crying."

"No, I know you are crying. Why are you crying?"

"Because."

Now, to be fair, I have had my fair share of those conversations with my "neurotypical" kids as well. The difference is *why* comes into focus a lot faster with them, even when they don't want to tell me why. It might take some time, but I can get there. With Nate, getting to why is like me trying to play the part of Sherlock Holmes without the cool English accent and sidekick doctor. You have to come at things sideways, obliquely, catch him off guard in the hopes that he will give up a string of clues you can put together. A childhood spent helping my father build and fix everything under the sun was preparation for that, I think.

When I do get to a why with Nate, it feels like a revelation. It doesn't always fix things, but it is wonderful just to get it. Like I said, we get the best stories.

For the life of us, we could not figure out what the deal with green tiles was. It was my mother who put two and two together. Nate loved playing Pac-Man World on the PlayStation 2. One of the obstacles in the game was green goo—fall into it and you die. And so, no green tiles.

There was a logic there. A why that I could not see, but Nathan could, even though he could not articulate it. It just wasn't my logic. My mother looked at the *what*s and connected the dots to come up with a *why*. The more I thought about it, the more it made sense. I've had to approach Nate the same way I did when learning from my dad how to fix things when I was a kid. I have since realized that Dad didn't always know what he was getting into when he started. What he did have was a basic mechanical understanding and a mind that observed things. He took things apart and looked at how they fit together—really looked. Remembered. Saw what didn't fit or what was worn out or whatever.

Sometimes you have to break things down into component parts to figure out how they fit together, to get to why.

I have always been a firm believer in starting with why. I think that it's the most fundamental human question and far too often we simply drift through life trying to keep ourselves busy or amused or whatever just so we don't have to face that question.

But sometimes we have to look at the end product before we can get to why. We have to slowly take things apart to get to the reason. I hate that. I want the answer now. Give me the rationale. Let me evaluate and decide if it's something that I want to spend my time and energy on.

No such luxury with a child. The why is hidden.

Every parent of an autistic child asks why. Why did this happen to my child? Why did this happen to me? Why, God? Why? (With alternating exasperation and rage, I find.)

I wish I had a good answer to that. I don't. But then, I haven't gotten to the finished product yet. And I'm not even sure if that finished product is Nate or if it's me. I'm guessing it's both. Sometimes there simply isn't a why, at least not one we can get to in the here and now.

In my self-pitying moments I wonder if God ever asks himself why about us. I have multiple theological degrees. I can give you the arguments and the clichés about God not being surprised by the dumb things that we do.

But then I think about Matthew's account of Jesus on the cross and that most disturbing question: "About three in the afternoon Jesus cried out in a loud voice, '*Eli, Eli, lema sabachthani?*' (which means 'My God, my God, why have you forsaken me?')" (Matthew 27:46, NIV).

Jesus asks why. He knows the answer. That's not the point. The point is that God himself, the second person of the Trinity, knows such extreme agony, such extreme suffering that he calls out, "WHY?!" to the Father.

For most of us, when it comes to our kids, when it comes to the pain in our spouses and all of the lost hopes and dreams, "why" is less about a good reason than it is a demand that this all matters somehow, that it means something. To be sure, we would like reasons too.

I am learning to come at why from new angles. And I am learning that sometimes why is less important than I thought. Sometimes you need to get in there and *do* even when you don't have all of the right answers or even half of the information that you feel like you need.

I would have never thought that years of oil and sawdust and hammers and wrenches and watching my father tear apart cars and rebuild garage doors from scratch—and well, a hundred other things I don't remember—would help me to understand my son. I never would have thought that it might take a son with autism to jump-start me from being paralyzed by why and start doing something.

Jesus asked the Father why.

The answer was us—was me.

Discussion Questions:

1. What are your whys?

2. When you ask why is it because you really want to know or is it out of exasperation and rage?

3. Do you trust that God has an answer to your whys even if you can't see it?

4. Where can you go for assurance?

Turning the Ship Around

BARBARA K. DITTRICH

Is there any such thing as Christians cheering each other up? Do you love me enough to want to help me? Does it mean anything to you that we are brothers in the Lord, sharing the same Spirit? Are your hearts tender and sympathetic at all? Then make me truly happy by loving each other and agreeing wholeheartedly with each other, working together with one heart and mind and purpose.

Philippians 2:1-2, TLB

As so often happens with our children, our daughter's diagnoses were revealed piece by piece over the years. Working with so many other parents, I know that we are not the only ones who have endured this incremental diagnosing. Too frequently, it seems like a process of elimination to get our children to the diagnosis and help that they need to live fully the life possible for them.

When we parents first realize things are not quite right, it can seem like we are trying to steer a huge ship that is hopelessly careening through violent waters, moving in the wrong direction. Speaking up and reaching out to others can make all the difference in turning the ship around. For some people that means medical intervention. For others, it can mean school intervention.

Our journey began in part when our daughter was in first grade. I had always known things were a bit different with our daughter than they were with my other two children. However, no educator seemed to find her unmanageable until her first-grade teacher.

It was a challenging year. As this teacher found coping difficult, things began to unravel. At the same time, I was having terrible knee troubles, followed by surgeries and major complications. Because the teacher did not do well with managing active first grade children, our daughter ended up in the emergency room at one point for X-rays because another child dropped her while giving her a piggyback ride. Finally, the teacher confronted me, asking me to have our daughter assessed for ADHD. I found myself in tears because my years of suspicions were being confirmed.

I took her to the pediatrician, and we had an assessment done, with the various educators and ourselves answering questionnaires. Of course, the process confirmed our daughter's ADHD. From that point forward, the teacher hounded me, asking if I had seen a doctor about getting our child on medication. Her pressure was not only inappropriate and illegal, but I had to assure her that it simply was not going to happen that school year because my own health situation was the priority.

The next school year, our daughter had not only been put on medication just prior to the school year, her teacher was also much more well-suited to her needs. As our daughter began to have allergic reactions to the various medications, the teacher even worked diligently with us to bring out the best in our little sprite during her second grade. This vivacious educator was engaging and helped our daughter to succeed.

It seemed we were working on an every-other-year schedule for helpful, well-suited teachers, because we found ourselves less encouraged by her third-grade teacher. Our daughter seemed to be having troubles with her teacher that year. She would frequently tell us of her instructor yelling at her and being mean to her.

At the same time, I was noticing some concerns at home. Given my professional experience, bells and whistles started to go off in my mind when she was screaming just from having her hair brushed. I knew I wasn't being as brutal with combing and brushing her hair as her response would seem to indicate.

All of this prompted me to speak to her principal, who ended up making all the difference in getting our girl's little ship turned around.

"Let's call an I-Team," the principal proclaimed. She seemed to have no second thoughts about bringing the various partners in the special education program together to listen to our concerns and help formulate a plan of attack. In the first meeting, we expressed our apprehensions along with the third-grade teacher disgustedly expressing hers.

"What makes me angry is that she's so darn smart," hissed her teacher.

Unfazed, the rest of the team fired off a variety of assessments that could be done. The speech therapist volunteered language tests to determine if our daughter's complete inability to write an essay was tied to language processing difficulties. The special education teacher jumped in with the IQ assessment. A battery of tests was suggested, and we were encouraged to get an independent assessment done by a neuropsychologist. It seemed liked a team problem-solving huddle where each had taken on their part of the assignment with eagerness, agreeing to reconvene when more information had been gathered.

While exhausting and heart-wrenching, it was still so incredibly gratifying to have a group of professionals willing to surround us and our daughter to get to the bottom of her difficulties. With the exception of the actual classroom teacher, each team member seemed so committed to our child and helping her reach her maximum potential. I had spoken with enough parents around the nation, who did not have that sort of warmth and cooperation from their local school, to know not to take our team's eager cooperation for granted.

As is always the case, the reams of paper generated by hours and hours of testing were overwhelming. Our heads were swimming from the intricate details of every assessment. The neuropsychological testing was particularly intense, with both the entire day of testing, along with the not-so-easy-to-hear interpretation of test results. Our heads hurt from all of the information.

Nevertheless, that was exactly what our team needed in order to start turning the ship around. Working together with one heart, mind, and purpose, the professionals at our daughter's elementary school put together a beautiful plan to help her overcome her obstacles. This included formulating a sensory diet with the occupational therapist, scheduling sensory breaks, introducing methods for reading quietly, providing special help with writing, as well as accommodations during regular classes.

It was incredibly heartening, especially because the third-grade teacher came into the meeting angry, with guns a-blazing.

"Do you know what your daughter wrote on her standardized testing?" she curled her lips, as she shook the papers at us.

We read the essay question for an article on dinosaurs that was part of the test. What was our daughter's response?

"Yeah, well, I already know all of this, so so long suckers!"

As we blushed in embarrassment, the room erupted with laughter.

"Yep, that's my girl!" proclaimed the behavior intervention specialist.

The teacher, still angry, had to be coaxed and convinced by the rest of the staff. We, on the other hand, could see how very much our girl was loved and accepted by the people at this school. Every single one of them loved her for the character she was. They saw great potential in her, not hopelessness. Each one seemed committed to making things work for our daughter. They felt these would be simple adaptations that could have major impact for our girl.

In her fourth-grade year, our daughter's individual education plan (IEP) was carried over from third grade and implemented. She was assigned to a first-year teacher with a loving and gentle spirit. While I had my fears about our daughter walking all over this young woman, the year was transformational. Our daughter made incredible strides because of the hard work and commitment of the special education team at our daughter's elementary school. She began consistently to read independently. She could craft a written narrative that reasonably collected her thoughts while authentically expressing her voice. She developed appropriate friendships. Her instructor was unflappable and calm in the face of our daughter's frequent erratic and disruptive behavior. The ship's direction had not only been righted, but we were moving full-steam ahead in the right direction.

After hearing so many stories of frustration and hopelessness in my job supporting parents raising children with special needs, I was finally able to see with my own eyes that a fantastic, cooperative special education team was possible. This is how it was intended to work. Because of our experience with these competent, compassionate, dedicated individuals, I was able to give other parents hope.

My message of encouragement to other parents would be this: You know your own child best. Do not deny the challenges that your child has. Do not let others define who your child is. Do speak up to get your child the best help available to them. Be unrelenting. Be your child's best advocate because no one else will do that job for them. Don't give up hope. Know that there are godly teams of dedicated special educators that will help build and execute an excellent IEP for your child. Persist until you find them.

Discussion Questions:

1. What was your first school experience with your remarkable child?

2. How did your child's team surprise you?

3. What has frustrated you in trying to move things in the right direction for your child?

4. How can you positively persevere and redeem your child's school challenges, whether they be social, academic, or both?

Never Let Go

KATHLEEN DEYER BOLDUC

And Jacob was left alone, and a man wrestled with him until the breaking of the day. When the man saw that he did not prevail against Jacob, he touched the hollow of his thigh; and Jacob's thigh was put out of joint as he wrestled with him. Then he said, 'Let me go, for the day is breaking.' But Jacob replied, 'I will not let you go, unless you bless me.'

Genesis 32:24-26, RSV

This morning, while practicing *lectio divina* (sacred reading of Scripture), I find myself wrestling with an angel of God. The verses are from Genesis—the story of Jacob wrestling with an angel on the fork of the Jabbok, as he prepares to return to his homeland, to the brother he had cheated out of their father's blessing many years before.

To give you the context of the story: Jacob is extremely nervous about the upcoming confrontation with his brother, Esau. Will Esau accept him? Forgive him? Or will Esau attack Jacob and the entire clan he's brought with him? Jacob divides his clan and the flocks of sheep, goats, cows and camels he's brought as gifts, into two camps. He sends them on ahead, hoping the gifts will appease his brother. Left alone for the last night of his long and arduous journey, he uses a stone as a pillow and tries to sleep.

> "...and a man wrestled with him until the breaking of the day. When the man saw that he did not prevail against Jacob, he touched the hollow of his thigh; and Jacob's thigh was put out

69

of joint as he wrestled with him. Then he said, "Let me go, for the day is breaking." But Jacob said, "I will not let you go, unless you bless me." And he said to him, "What is your name?" And he said, "Jacob." Then he said, "Your name shall no more be called Jacob, but Israel, for you have striven with God and with men, and have prevailed." Then Jacob asked him, "Tell me, I pray, your name." But he said, "Why is it that you ask my name?" And there he blessed him. So Jacob called the name of the place Peniel, saying, "For I have seen God face to face, and yet my life is preserved." The sun rose upon him as he passed Penu'el, limping because of his thigh. Therefore to this day the Israelites do not eat the sinew of the hip which is upon the hollow of the thigh, because he touched the hollow of Jacob's thigh on the sinew of the hip." (Gen 32:24-32, RSV)

One verse grabs me and will not let me go: "I will not let you go, unless you bless me." This is what I'd like to say to God! And so, I take the words with me into meditation, repeating them as a centering prayer.

I will not let you go, unless you bless me. I will not let you go, unless you bless me. I will not let you go, unless you bless me.

Usually, it takes several minutes to reach a place within myself that is quiet enough to hear the still, small voice of God. Often, that voice is just a feeling, or a distant, lovely melody. Today, God reaches immediately through my restless mind, the chatter of cicadas, and the cat purring as he twines himself around my legs. God grabs me by the shoulders and gently shakes me, as a father gently shakes a child who will not listen. "Look at me. I'm talking to you. Listen to what I'm saying."

I listen. This is what I hear:

"Kathy, you have been wrestling with me for thirty-three years. You wrestled with me after your father died, through those long months and years of your grief. You wrestled with me as you

70

learned to mother your sons. Remember how you didn't feel adequate to the task?

"You began wrestling with me in earnest when Joel was only a few days old. You wrestled with me through the jaundice, the decision to begin physical therapy and speech therapy, and the decision to enroll him in a preschool for children with disabilities. We wrestled through his diagnosis at age three, and again at age five. We wrestled through all of those IEP meetings, through the decision to take him out of public school and enroll him in the county school.

"We wrestled through so many behaviors—the times you locked yourself in the bathroom to keep safe from his hands, stood outside of the car on the side of the road as he kicked the windows, and as he pulled the hair of strangers on the street. We wrestled as you and Wally took turns staying up with him all night when he couldn't sleep.

"You wrestled with me when your love for him was so great you felt it would burst when you watched him worship with abandon, giving joy to all who watched. We wrestled as you found the courage to try the DAN protocol, and as he found success at Beckman Adult Center. We wrestled as you and Wally made the difficult decision to move Joel from your home to Safe Haven Farms. We've wrestled these last two years through his difficult transition.

"We've wrestled through doctor visit after doctor visit, hospitalization after hospitalization. We've wrestled through this newest transition to the day program at Liberty Center.

"You've wrestled with me through your other sons' issues, difficulties in your marriage, and through your mother's decline into the confusion of dementia.

"Do you see a pattern here, Kathy? You've never let me go. You've held on tight. You've never once let go. Even when I touched your hip and the pain made walking difficult, you did not let go. Through the wrestling you've become strong. In order to keep on wrestling with me you stepped out of the dark cupboard of lies where you once hid, afraid of the truth. And what is that truth? You are my beloved daughter. I created you for a purpose. I give you the power to speak my truth wherever you go.

"And so in the midst of the struggle, I give you a new name. Truth Teller.

"I know you are tired, Kathy. The wrestling can stop. Go forth. Stand tall in your newfound strength. Tell everyone you meet that I love them. Tell them that I want to wrestle with them as a father wrestles with his children. Tell them that I walk with them in the midst of their struggles and pain.

"Tell them not to give up."

Oh Lord, I thank you and praise you for never once letting me go. Thank you for loving me enough to not only accept my struggles, but to engage directly with me in the midst of those struggles. Lord, you never once let me go. Give me the courage to stand straight and tall in this new role you've given me. Let me live up to the name of Truth Teller. Let it be the truth of your unfailing love that I share with others who wrestle still in the midst of disability.

Discussion Questions:

1. Looking back at your life with autism, where are those places that you have wrestled with God?

2. Have you ever felt like giving up? What (or who) encouraged you to hang on for the ride?

3. If God were to give you a new name today, what would it be?

Have This Mind Among You: The Gift of Empathy

MICHELE BOVELL

Let each of you look not only to his own interests, but also to the interests of others. Have this mind among yourselves, which is yours in Christ Jesus....
Philippians 2:4-5, ESV

I was a loner as a young child growing up in Jamaica, and were it not for my imagination, I would have been lonely, too. My days were spent in solitary play, lost in thought, and shared with lizards, feral cats, and our dogs. And there was Maurice. He was my first best friend, an imaginary friend almost, entering my silent world of play, standing in as father, brother, son, sidekick, and patient. Gentle and silent, he lent his body as a canvas upon which I projected the characters of my daydreams.

It was said, and Jamaican stories always descend into the fanciful, that as a child he was happy and developed normally, but when his mother abandoned the family, grief caused an immediate arrest in his mental development, so that twenty years later, he found in this lonesome preschooler with her dolly and geckos a fitting playmate.

Maurice's disability was never defined, nor did it matter to anyone. We lived in that sort of culture where the line was drawn sharply between those considered acceptable and those rejected by society. Marijuana addiction, intellectual delay, Down Syndrome,

75

nervous breakdown, all landed one in the broad category of "mad" or "not right" if one wanted to be generous. But Maurice's differences—this Chinese man, so tall and childlike—made him a lovely curiosity to me.

Eventually, Maurice and his father would move away from our community. As the years passed, and he would return to visit, he would seem smaller, less my peer, more a little brother to amuse and be amused by and from whom to accept his little gifts and attention. He was a fixture in my childhood, and with him, an attraction to those who were different and vulnerable. In the years that followed, that friendship revealed itself to be part of a larger storyline, for disability would come even closer to home when two of my own sons' development would arrest, and I would watch the gap widen as the milestones ticked away.

There were many things on my mind when I returned home to Jamaica decades later, now a wife and mother in my late thirties. High among them was seeing Maurice again, who had moved back into the white house across the street with his father. Another was to visit my old elementary school. Quite incidentally, I had come across an image on the web of the signage outside the school: "Harbour View School" and above that, scribbled by hand in black paint as though an afterthought, "Asenath E. Nelson Special Education Uni.". The day after our arrival, my mother and I made our way down the hill toward the sea and into the schoolyard full of children screaming at play. Passing by familiar classrooms, through the open cafeteria, and by the bank of drinking faucets, we made our way to the very back of the building to what was once the old woodshop room. There, while everyone else frolicked outdoors at lunchtime, sat a dozen quiet children and their three teachers.

We entered and introduced ourselves, and immediately the children flocked around us, absorbing our hugs and attention and excited to meet someone from "farrin" (foreign/overseas). Some had mild facial abnormalities, others showed familiar characteristics of Down syndrome, one boy had high functioning autism, and a few others seemed quite typically functioning— boys, perhaps sent there for repeated disruptions in class. The classroom was a catchall—any and every challenge placed together. (I don't recall such a place when I was a student there. Apart from that one "mad" boy a year ahead of me in school, I knew of no child with special needs in the public-school system in Jamaica when I was a child.) The teachers spoke to us of their limited resources, and we promised to do what we could to return with basic supplies for the children. But my eyes kept shifting from the women to the child clutching blocks in a corner on the floor.

His name was Kurtis, and the women overseeing the classroom knew only enough to explain that he was severely autistic. His teachers, untrained regarding autism, and afraid of the child's behavior, had insisted that he be sedated to attend school. His parents, extremely poor, were uneducated regarding their child's condition and their options. They had been given only a diagnosis when he was a toddler, and this classroom had been the first and only resource made available to them, and so they complied with the school's demands. My heart broke for him. He did not belong here. None of them did, but especially not one so vulnerable and misunderstood. From that moment, Kurtis never left my heart and life, becoming like a sixth son to me.

We returned home after our vacation, but I felt compelled to revisit the island with my husband within a few months.

Leaving our children on the spectrum for the first time in their lives, we returned bearing as many books and resources as we could to educate and equip his mother. She and Kurtis met us at our hotel, and together we taught her as much as we could about autism—about language delay and motor skills deficits, about sensory integration dysfunction and sensory diets, about nutrition and food intolerance. Whatever we had learned over the years, we poured into this overwhelmed woman and her son. We brushed his skin and massaged his joints, and when he had had enough of us and took off running through the lobby of the hotel and down the beach, we pursued him and taught her how to calm him. All the while, we were falling in love with this young boy the same age as our Ethan. When we returned home, my husband and I worked to remove him from that school and to locate and see him placed in an environment more appropriate for the level of care he needed. Kurtis remains an important part of our lives today, he will always be, and we count his gains among God's good gifts to us.

Before stepping into that classroom and meeting Kurtis, it had become so easy to remain absorbed in our own struggle as parents of children with disabilities—to consider ourselves always in the position to be the object of others' assistance, prayers, and concern. Disability became an exemption from Christian love in action—we were recipients of grace, but rarely a means of grace in the lives of others who were suffering. Kurtis opened a doorway out of preoccupation with my own children's needs, and with my challenges as their caregiver. His presence in my life opened my eyes to see suffering often missed, and as with Maurice before him, to more fully identify with and see beauty and worth in those who society fails to value.

It took seven years of love and steady involvement with Kurtis and his family, of consistently pointing to Christ, and of mining with them for evidence of his grace in their lives, but the day came when Evelyn announced that she and Kurtis' father had accepted Christ and were making plans to marry. The Word of God calls us to "look not only to [our] own interests, but also to the interests of others" (Philippians 2:4, ESV). It's not just our Christian duty, but our heritage: "Have this mind among yourselves, which *is* yours in Christ Jesus" (Philippians 2:5, ESV). Through word and deed, we proclaim Christ and who we are in him. We imitate Christ as the grace of God enables us, in the midst of our own pain, to care for others who are suffering. In doing so, in dying to ourselves for the sake of others, we become a visual representation of Christ to those in desperate search of Hope.

Kurtis entered our lives amid what we term the *lean years*— a time when we ourselves lacked supports and resources for our own children and had few empathetic friendships and little fellowship as parents. At a time when we were tempted to despair of our own situation, joy and hope came quite unexpectedly through self-forgetfulness.

Discussion Questions

1. Has the very real struggle of parenting a child on the spectrum sensitized you to suffering, or has it so narrowed your focus that you no longer see those around you who are hurting?

2. What are practical ways that you can begin to "look to the interests of others" within the disability community?

Warrior Parents

DEBORAH ABBS

The Lord will fight for you; you need only to be still.

Exodus 14:14, NIV

I really should have taken up kickboxing, or just plain old boxing, or something involving a punching bag. I guess I still could. If I'd known all the fighting—or what some prefer to call "advocating"—I would need to do for my son Luke, I just might have.

Luke had just turned three when he was diagnosed with autism, and that meeting with Dr. Davis, the neuropsychologist, was devastating. My mom came with me that day because Mike had to work, and I remember how mom and I wanted a plan: "Do XYZ and he will get better." The doctor did give us a plan that included preschool through the school district, Applied Behavior Analysis (ABA) and speech therapy (Luke was talking at that point), but she said it was hard to say what the results would be. After many tears on my part and much reassurance and what I thought was denial on Mike's part (see his vignette, "The Other Side of Suffering,"—I was wrong about that!), I hit the ground running. ABA, check. Special needs preschool, check. Speech therapy, check. Back then I didn't realize that becoming a warrior parent would be required.

Instead of gaining more speech (he had about seventy-five words and some two word phrases from age two to about three), Luke began losing speech until we were down to one word: More! And then that disappeared too. He's non-verbal now although we do hear from him occasionally. When he is mad, we often hear a loud "NO!"

His experience in Batavia school district's early childhood program was awesome. We were so thankful for his team there and that they had a class specifically for kids with autism. His teacher, Korin, was especially knowledgeable and willing to be creative, and his aid, Terri, was super patient even when Luke would lash out and bite. So kindergarten came as a complete shock—and not in a good way.

Before school started that fall we set up a time for Luke and me to visit the classroom. This was a classroom specifically for children with autism and it was run through a co-op of another school district. His room had a new teacher. Luke needed to at least see the place, in order to help ease his transition to a new building with all new people. I brought along his home ABA therapist, and she typed up basic notes about the programs Luke was working on at home. Luke did really well not running wild and actually sat at the table for a few minutes, but I knew we were in trouble when his teacher said, "I'm so glad you brought me this information. I really have no clue what I'm doing."

Um. What? Come again?

And I'm sending my precious boy to your class, why?

When we walked out of the room, Ana (his home therapist) and I looked at each other with wide eyes, and she diplomatically said, "Well, that was interesting . . ." Right when I got back home, I flew to the computer and sent an email off to the director of the program asking her what this teacher's qualifications were. She asked me to give his teacher a little time to learn. Prior to teaching this *kindergarten* class, she had been an aid for *adults* with disabilities. Stupidly, I agreed—not a good move. It turned out to be a place where Luke and the other children weren't taught *anything*. Where none of the plans were followed, no IEP upheld, and no data taken. This whole experience was such a surprise because my nephew, Teddy, who also has autism, has had a good experience with the same co-op. But so much depends on which classroom teacher your child gets and what their experience and training entail.

So it was time for some fighting on my part. And I wish I had stepped in the ring sooner.

Finally, in February, after a tip from a friend whose son was in the same class, we hired an advocate and got him out of there. In April of his kindergarten year, we placed him at a school for students with autism called Giant Steps, for which our school district pays. It's a much better place where the staff is actually trained in how to work with folks with autism. Luke has high sensory needs, and we so appreciate that he can take a body sock walk around the building or roller skate. They even have a squeeze machine, like the one Temple Grandin built.

But this didn't mean my fighting days were over.

He wasn't making progress with the Picture Exchange Communication System (PECS) at Giant Steps. Much of this had to do with the fact that the physical pictures distracted him; he liked to play with them, stim with them, or chew on them. We got Luke an iPad, and his home ABA team worked with him so that he learned to point to things and play games on there. We decided to meet with the Giant Steps staff and the tech person for our school district because we wanted the school district to provide an iPad for Luke on which to play educational games and, then, to use for communication. His school team didn't think he could do it. He'd tried to use an iPad at school, but he had only stimmed on it. Why? He loves crinkly things, and the school iPad had a crinkly cover that was waterproof.

So it was time for more advocating.

I told them, "He's distracted by the cover on there."

"That's the kind we use," the school replied.

Cheryl, his home Board Certified Behavior Analyst (BCBA) also tried, "I'm sure there is another protective case option that won't be so distracting for him."

The school doubled down, "But that's the one we use."

You get the picture.

The district said they would pay for an iPad for him on a trial basis. Reluctantly, the school allowed him to use a different case. Guess what. He learned to play games on the iPad. Guess what else. Now he has a PECS app on the iPad that he is using to communicate!

I love the television show "Parenthood." Kristina Braverman, one of the characters on the show, has a son, Max, who is on the autism spectrum. Watching one episode, I got teary when she said this about caring for a child with autism: "What works for some kids doesn't work for all kids. . . . I feel like the system is broken. . . My husband and I have fought the system time and time again to make sure he gets what he needs, that he's not overlooked. . . . My son, Max, is a fighter. . . . On behalf of Max, I've become a fighter, too."

For those of us whose loved one is nonverbal, I think we feel what Braverman describes even more acutely. Since Luke can't talk and tell me what is going on, it's a huge act of faith to entrust him with others, when I'm not with him. If I find out that something is off in the way he's treated, my mama-bear response can be quite loud and aggressive. But isn't it true that we stand up for those we love, just like God fights for us?

One of the hardest, most emotional battles to fight can actually be with our churches. Thankfully, our church is growing in the area of special needs ministry, but not without tears and struggles littering the path. It hurts.

Jesus reached out to those on the margins. He spent time with them, healed them, and had compassion on them. Each of His children is an important part of His body, and He wants them to be able to use the gifts He has given them. When His children with special needs are missing—in some sad cases even asked to stop coming to church—His body is incomplete. It's a huge mess and really tough when the church is slow to follow His lead. When the families who need extra support and love are rejected, it makes me so mad and so sad.

When I remember that the Lord fights for me, it's an immense help as I do battle for Luke, both inside and outside of the church. The Lord fights for us. As Moses led the Israelites out of slavery, they were terrified that the Egyptians were pursuing them. Moses reminded them to stand firm because God would fight for them. And He did! He used Moses to part the Red Sea so that the Israelites could escape. If you have time, take a moment and read all of Exodus 14.

Jesus is the one doing battle for us and our special needs loved ones. We are not duking it out on our own, even if it feels that way sometimes. He is in our corner, and He has not forgotten us. We are not alone in the fight. *Thank you, Lord, for that!*

Discussion Questions:

1. Have you had to do battle for your child on the spectrum? If so, how has it changed you?

2. Is it easy or tough for you to remember that the Lord is fighting for you and your child/children? Why?

3. Re-read Exodus 14:14. What do you think it means "to be still" in this verse?

Her Brothers' Keeper

KELLI RA ANDERSON

To all who mourn in Israel, he will give a crown of beauty for ashes, a joyous blessing instead of mourning, festive praise instead of despair. In their righteousness, they will be like great oaks that the LORD has planted for his own glory.

Isaiah 61:3, NLT

The day my five-year-old daughter came bursting through our front room door, breathlessly demanding that I make her older brother stop calling her a bad name, I braced myself for the worst. What "bad word" had finally found its way into my children's vocabulary?

"He called me a Canadian!" she cried indignantly. "A what?" I asked, thinking I hadn't heard this right. "A Canadian!" she repeated, stamping her foot to punctuate her outrage, short ponytails shaking along with her rising temper.

Before I could respond, the door flew open again. This time, her older brother shouted out his defense, "I did not! I did not call her a Canadian!"

Okay, what on earth was I missing here? What was the deal with Canadians? Other than the regrettable importation of Justin Bieber, what was so unforgiveable?

"I called her a *comedian!*"

"See? See? That's what he called me!" she shot back, vindicated. Canadian or comedian, it was all the same insult to her.

I burst out laughing (not a good thing to do, we have since learned, when our daughter is being serious), only fanning the flame of her outrage, until I was able to convince her that her honor had not been besmirched.

Like most siblings, my kids have had their share of arguments over the years. But unlike most of our friends and neighbors' families, our daughter has endured things most of her friends would never understand. Although she is the youngest of our three, all two years apart, she is in many ways our oldest, because her brothers are on the spectrum.

Like so many neurotypical siblings of disability, the presence of autism in our family's life has meant that, by necessity, our daughter has experienced a childhood in which autism has required more of our time, our money, and our emotional reserve. It has been a life that, in spite of all our efforts to make it otherwise, has been patently unfair.

Enduring an almost steady diet of parenting attention deficit, combined with the frequent stresses of her brothers' meltdowns, public awkward moments in both her school and our neighborhood, and the injustice of inequitable discipline in which more is expected of the younger than the older, you might conclude our daughter would become angry and resentful and well within her rights to demand a different family.

She has.

Truthfully, at times, we have all wanted to run away (boys included). But like anything we finally lay at God's feet and beg Him to redeem, God redeems our family's life with this disorder. And I am witnessing His redemptive work that creates something beautiful in all our lives—especially my daughter's.

Like Jesus, who often would walk away from the never-ending needs of the crowds, we learned that we, too, must get away from the stresses of our daily lives to tank up on peace and quiet. For our daughter, it meant finally giving back to her a small fraction of what has so often been denied: our exclusive attention and our time.

Last week, she and I boarded a train for an overnight trip to Chicago to stay in the swanky and historic Palmer House Hotel. True, an overnight trip to the Windy City during an arctic Midwestern winter is no two-week vacation to the balmy breezes of the Caribbean. But for our wearied hearts and minds, it was just what the doctor ordered.

For two days, we were on the town, discovering the magical combination of tapioca pearls and frozen yogurt, rolling our eyes at the ridiculous prices on the Magnificent Mile, risking life and limb in city taxis, and entertaining our inner geeks by exploring ancient Egypt and dinosaurs at the Field Museum. Most importantly, we laughed, we ate, and we slept without a care in the world. We needed that. She needed that.

There have been times, however, we needed help beyond the reach of a train ticket. There have been times as parents, traveling an often unknown path while dealing with disability, we were so lost and our family dynamics so frayed we sought the help of additional family counseling. Like the canary in the coal mine, Sarah's health alerted us that we needed more help.

Kicking and screaming (thankfully, not literally), she joined our family of five as we trudged into a counselor's office, needing a professional's perspective to help us see what our eyes could not. These sessions enable us to recognize the causes of some stresses in our daughter's life and to plan a strategy to relieve them as best we can, both, critical to helping her stay the course.

She is old enough now, however, at the sage old age of fourteen, to verbalize something I never thought I would hear. She really does love her brothers and cares deeply for them. When they all attended the same school, she did not want to be around them—that time in a child's life when jostling for an identity and a place in the world can become a social quagmire she was only just beginning to learn to navigate. She came through these years all the stronger, more confident in who she is and less willing to give into the dictates of her culture or her peers.

Now in high school, Sarah invites her brothers to eat at the same table with her and her friends, she advises them on what to say around their peers, and she often will volunteer to go with them in social settings where adult help is too conspicuous. Although we never asked her to step into this role, she is becoming in many ways her older brothers' keeper.

More importantly, her life with her brothers has translated into a compassion that goes beyond our family. While my daughter suffered in ways I never would have wanted, God is redeeming and using it, teaching her to be a blessing to others in return. Beauty out of ashes.

As is so often the case with those who endure hardship, God transforms the hardship into a sensitive heart. For Sarah, a life with autism taught her to read the telltale signs of a child's struggle with disability that compels her to include those on the outside.

Being a gifted extrovert and diving into social settings where others fear to tread, she is learning how to use her social equity to become the bridge across which socially-challenged kids can walk to better connect with their neurotypical peers.

Also an artist, with a long history of keeping our household in a constant state of paper shortage, she currently is exploring her options for a career that might combine her love of art with her desire to work with disabled children and teens. Of course, college is still a few years away, and God only knows the direction He has in mind for her future. But as of today, we couldn't be more proud of our daughter and the young woman she is.

Discussion Questions:

1. In what ways is God bringing beauty from ashes in your family's life with disability?

2. What characteristics of strength do you see in yourself or in your children that are a result of your experiences together?

3. Where do you still need to be in prayer for healing for the hardships the stresses of family life can cause in your family members?

4. Do you need to consider additional help or strategies to help ensure the emotional health of all your children?

5. Do you see ways in which your family's struggles can, in turn, become an encouragement to others in more difficult circumstances?

Lions and Tigers and Emotions and the Future, Oh My!

KEVIN O'BRIEN

Rejoice in the Lord always. I will say it again: Rejoice! Let your gentleness be evident to all. The Lord is near. Do not be anxious about anything, but in every situation, by prayer and petition, with thanksgiving, present your requests to God. And the peace of God, which transcends all understanding, will guard your hearts and your minds in Christ Jesus.

Philippians 4:4-7, NIV

Philippians 4:6 often strikes me as trite. Especially when I think about the concerns that my wife has about our son. And in the quiet moments, the moments when I am contemplating or writing and am forced to confront my own concerns: "Be anxious for nothing." How ridiculous can you be? Have you really lived in this world, Paul? Do you really hear yourself? Please. Puh-lease! He said to the man who has been jailed and shipwrecked, scourged and more. I've read 2 Corinthians 11:24-27. He can keep that list. And he wins the suffering contest. Hands down. And still our fear and suffering is real. And it is hard to move past it. We worry about our children.

When Nate was about three we lived in a townhouse complex. We were one row from the park and about a block over. Nate loved the park. LOVED it. One day he got out, snuck out really, and went to the park. We didn't know that of course. We just knew that he was gone. And we were frantic with worry. That

93

pit in the stomach kind of worry. He really didn't talk much at the time, but his laser focus was already in play. If he was on a mission, good luck getting him to break his concentration for silly little things like parental concern. I remember calling him. About ten minutes of panic. Then hearing someone ask if we were looking for a little boy. Yes! He's at the park. Relief. Gratitude. Running. Hugs to a bewildered child—what's all the fuss about? And anger. I think it's about as close as Loretta and I have come to having the same emotion in a situation.

I can't say from experience what a mom thinks about when she worries about her autistic child. I think I know from observing my wife and some friends. But I don't know viscerally. I can't get in my wife's skin to feel what she feels. Our concerns overlap of course. It's not like we're a different species (insert standard comedian joke here), or that we don't talk about these things.

But I know she worries most about different sorts of things than I do. How will he get along with those around him? Will he be able to have "normal" relationships? What kinds of things will he be able to do?

Very early on in our journey into the world of autism I said something really stupid. Out loud in front of someone that we really didn't know, I stated that Nate would probably never move out of our house or get married.

I probably was not wrong. I still think that this is likely to be true, but I was certainly not wise in my approach. I had not talked to Loretta beforehand about this assessment. I had not given her the time to process this idea. It's not exactly what anyone wants for their child. Getting blindsided by a momentous thing like that in a public space, well, let's just say it was not my finest hour.

I wonder if it's harder for moms emotionally than for dads. Upon reflection, I think that times like those settle the question for me. I recently had a conversation about this very issue. Three different families with autistic children, the same response. For mom, the diagnosis hit like the proverbial ton of bricks. For dad, not so much. It's not that the diagnosis wasn't hard or that there was no emotion at all, but it was different. Not better. Not worse. Just different. In my own experience, when I heard autism linked to Nate for the first time it was like the puzzle pieces finally fit. I didn't particularly like the image on the puzzle, but at least I could make sense of it. It was much more traumatic for my wife.

I have heard the stories of dad's retreating into their jobs after a diagnosis of autism, of leaving mom to deal with the day-to-day hard stuff, the practical realities of life with an autistic child. It hasn't been my experience, but I don't doubt that it happens. I suppose that I do not do as much of the day-to-day, around the house that I should, but it really has nothing to do with Nate's autism. I was going to give a list of reasons, but they really sound like just so many excuses when I do, and it misses the point anyway.

Here's what I do know.

Dads worry about the future just as much as moms do. We just do it differently. I'll be honest. I don't worry about Nate's relationships as much as Loretta does. I worry about logistics. I worry about where and how he will live. Where the money will come from. Who will take care of him when we can't. I worry about the same things that I worry about every day—taking care of my family. Making sure that they have a house and food and the opportunity for a future. But the equation changes when a child on the spectrum is added. The math that ordinarily would do the trick no longer works. The calculus gets more complicated.

I can't say that this fact accounts for the stories of men retreating into their jobs, but I know it's a contributing factor. It can't not be. It's basically a truism in our culture that men are not as emotionally aware as women. It is probably true, but maybe, just maybe, the differences in the way that we process emotions are there to help us. Perhaps these differences mean that together we help one another process and cope; we strengthen where the other is weak. We cause the other to see what they cannot. Perhaps our differences can truly help each other and our children.

I ache for those who are going it alone on the journey of autism. Of the moms, and probably a few dads (but mostly moms), who do not have the support of a spouse who is there for them, of those who do not have the support and care of family. I do not know how we would have made it without that. We would have, but I am really not sure how.

The older I get, and the more that I study the Scriptures, the more that I realize that verse numbers get in the way as much as they help us. We look them up, find what we want, and move on, often missing the real point. We cannot take Philippians 4:6 alone. It is not a formula or abstraction. It is a part of a larger thought. A life characterized by worship, an attitude of gentleness, remembering the reality of the Lord's nearness, prayer. All of these are connected to the command not to be anxious. And not just any prayer. Petitions. Thankfulness.

These are not easy things when life is difficult. But they are still necessary. Peace does not come to us in abstraction. We want God to just drop it down on our heads, with no work, no change on our part. But life doesn't work that way. And it shouldn't. We have to get our orientation right first.

None of us come to life's problems in the same ways. Our angle of approach can't be the same because we are different people. Perhaps men tend to come from the same general direction and women from another. But even then we are not all the same. But it doesn't matter. Not really. Because where we are coming from is far less important than where we are facing.

Most of us face inward. Self is the center of our universe even when we are caring for our autistic children. We need to be facing God first. Rejoice in the Lord always! It's impossible when facing inwards. It's impossible not to be anxious in our situations.

I am trying to remember that it is only when I focus on God first that peace is even possible. I may not have the emotional worries that my wife does, but I have often lived a life of low-grade angst, even before Nate. And I cannot get rid of that angst on my own. It is only when I get off of self and reorient my life toward God that peace is possible.

I have no idea how Nate can go to college or get married or have a career. These are all things that simply don't seem to be in the cards—at least not as I read them.

Nate would disagree. He has plans for the future. College. A wife. Kids. A career (though I am honestly not sure what he thinks that means). To Nate the future is full of things that everyone just does. He doesn't worry about those things. Instead he worries about things that we find silly. Being late. Not getting to participate in a club. Approaching routine tasks or games in a way that he thinks is wrong.

All of us have our worries. All of us need to remember that it is focusing on God that gives us peace. I am trying to teach Nathan to pray when he is upset or worried. To ask Jesus to help him to calm down, to cope with the things that bother him. I am learning from my own teaching. I am learning to put God first. To be gentle when I am not naturally. I am learning to pray more honestly. To present petitions with thanksgiving, not just laundry lists.

I have not arrived. I am on a journey. Nate's presence in my life has helped me to see the person that God is calling me to be. As I move toward God, I find that I am worrying less. Who knows what the future holds for Nate. It is mine to do what I can; it is God's to care for him when I cannot. The question is whether or not I trust God to do so.

Discussion Questions:

1. What does worry, as it relates to your child on spectrum, look like for you? How is it different for your spouse?

2. Has the difference between your spouse's response and yours caused tension? If so, how can you work to resolve it?

3. Is peace an abstract concept for you or a reality?

4. How can you change your perspective from inward facing worry to Godward facing petition and thanksgiving?

Transformation on the Trail

KATHLEEN DEYER BULDOC

Don't copy the behavior and customs of this world, but let God transform you into a new person by changing the way you think. Then you will learn to know God's will for you, which is good and pleasing and perfect.
Romans 12:2, NLT

Golden sunlight streams through a canopy of beech, sycamore, and maple trees as my husband Wally, son Joel, and I walk through a splendid cathedral of light. It's Sunday, and we've decided to take an after-church hike at Hueston Woods State Park, just down the road from our home. It is the last week of October, and the trees are in full color. We couldn't have chosen a more beautiful day.

All of our senses are bombarded as we walk—leaf mold tickles our nostrils, leaves crunch underfoot, and above us, brittle, brown sycamore leaves applaud the day. A taste of smoke sits on the tongue as a wood fire burns in the nearby campground. A wild flutter erupts in my chest as thousands of grackles take flight in front of us, their feathers flashing purple and black against a patchwork of blue sky.

We hike single file. Leading the way, I am exhausted and moody despite the beauty of the day. I almost declined when Wally suggested a hike, but I felt a yearning to soak in this gorgeous day before autumn turns to winter. It disappears so quickly, this splendiferous glory of autumn. I know it could disappear overnight with the first passing storm.

Behind me, Joel, our youngest son, walks slowly and tentatively through the leaves. He has balance issues and is afraid of tripping on a root. Wally brings up the rear. Joel's manic chatter has subsided, and we are quiet. Our feet do the talking as we scuff across the yellow-carpeted forest floor.

I hear Joel's footsteps quicken, and turn from my ruminations on the fleeting nature of time to see him approaching at a near run. Surprised, I stop. He grabs my hand, looks me in the eye, grins, and pulls me forward. I wait for him to drop my hand, as he always does, but instead he squeezes it and swings my arm, his grin widening at my delight. For a moment, it feels so right, his hand a perfect fit in mine. A jolt of joy shocks my body. This is what my dreams are made of, this kind of connection with my son—dreams of eye-to-eye contact, deep conversations, arm-in-arm walks through the woods.

This full-body joy is answered, almost immediately, by my mind, which says, *no, don't go there*. My logical mind tells me there are no happy endings with twenty-six-year-old sons with autism. There is no happily-ever-after when they move away from home and you are left, not with "this is the way it's supposed to be," but with guilt, and sleepless nights, and often, regret.

And yet, here we are in a dream-come-true scenario. Joel holds my hand tight, matches my gait stride for stride, steals sideways gazes, his eyes playful, a smile flitting, now-you-see-it-now-you-don't, across his handsome face. *He is perfectly beautiful*, my heart sings.

Joy and sorrow play tug-of-war in my heart.

For a month Joel has been constant motion, constant chatter. He lashes out at staff with his hands, sometimes his feet. He spends hour upon hour walking or running around Safe Haven Farms, the sixty-acre farm for adults with autism that we helped to establish—where he now resides. No one can stop him from walking. I worry about his feet, which are cracked and blistered. My heart breaks as his anxiety escalates and erupts into aggression. I sit through behavior meetings once a week, where the aggression is charted. Manic swings, which we thought he'd left behind for good with a gluten-dairy free diet and a change of medication, are manifesting again, keeping him awake at night. Unable to sleep, he knocks on the doors of his housemates, waking them, as well. Everyone in his house on edge, waiting for behaviors to erupt, with no one sleeping soundly.

Dreams die hard. Our third son's adulthood will never be what we expected. We think we've moved through depression and anger, denial and guilt into a place called acceptance when yet another transition takes place and we grieve all over again. Letting go of this son is nothing like letting his big brothers Matt and Justin go. That was the natural, normal progression of life; it was something to celebrate, knowing we did our jobs as parents, giving them roots and wings. This feels like an amputation, so deep is this son's need, so intensive our care-giving, more than a quarter century's worth.

Joel's hand, still clutching mine, is warm and sweaty. I leave my doubting mind behind for a moment. Allow myself to totally inhabit this present moment. Become pure body, pure hand, pure connection.

Friends tell me I must cut the cord, not hold so tight to this beautifully whole yet broken boy-man. But this connection—

this fleshly hand in mine—tells me what my gut already knows. This cord is a living cord, a cord of flesh-and-blood. Unlike an umbilical cord, this cord can never be severed. Yes, like the towering maples, beech, and sycamore along this trail, we will experience all of the seasons of life. We have known green and growing times, and we will experience them again. We have lived through times of autumnal beauty that signaled the end of an era, and we will know them again. We have suffered and waited through fallow seasons where it seemed as if nothing would ever grow again, like this past year, with Joel's move away from home, a seeming death for him, for me, for his father.

Every October I mourn the passing of autumn's glory. Dread the dark, dank days of winter to come. Today I want to stay pure hand, hold onto this moment forever. But my heart calls me to remember that spring always follows winter. Spring, when the sap flows upward, bringing with it new life, new sweetness, new possibilities, new ways of being.

This is what is true: I am Joel's mother. He is my son. And we are walking up a hill, hand in hand, through sunlight streaming golden through a canopy of maple, sycamore, and beech.

Nothing, unless I allow it, can rob me of this present joy. I choose joy.

Discussion Questions:

1. In what situation today might God be calling you to change the way that you think?

2. Joy and sorrow often play tug-of-war in our hearts when we parent children with autism. Which is winning the game in your life today? Read Psalm 42, and take your sorrow before the Lord,

ending with a time of praise. You might even want to write your own psalm.

3. Reflect on a time of "winter" in your life on the spectrum, and then reflect on the "spring" that followed. What flowers bloomed in that particular springtime? Write them down on a notecard, and tuck the notecard in your Bible so that you may revisit it on dark days.

The Heart of the Father

RICK BOVELL

Blessed be the God and Father of our Lord Jesus Christ, who has blessed us in Christ with every spiritual blessing in the heavenly places....

Ephesians 1:3, ESV

He was trying to drown the sounds of the vacuum's voice with his own. Without looking, I knew his hands were on his ears. I needed no great intuition as I had seen it scores of times before. But cleaning the house was necessary, and so was Daniel's discomfort—or was it? For some reason, I decided to try something different: With the vacuum in my right hand, I beckoned to Daniel with my left. Still wailing, he came. I took his right hand from his ear and placed it on the handle of the dreaded, loud monster. He now controlled the monster, and he liked it. Fear and fuss faded into the proud bearing of the conquering hero that all boys want to be. That night was the last night of seeing his hands on his ears (at least regarding the vacuum). Small victories are still victories, and each is a point at which I must stop and thank my Father.

Calling God "my Father" is not just a good theological phrase for me. I grew up without a dad in my home, and when I finally realized what I had been missing (I didn't truly realize until I was 20), the fatherhood of God became something that I treasured. I recognized that throughout my life he had been there, guiding and helping me. As a "fatherless" black boy the statistics were against me, but my Father intervened. I loved my Father and wanted to know him better, so I studied his Book. In examining Ephesians Chapter 1, I found four major ways that he expresses his fatherhood: he sees his children, he sacrificed for his children, he serves his children, and he schools his children.

Ephesians 1:4-5 (ESV) presents the Father as one who sees his children: "even as he (the Father) chose us in him (Christ) before the foundation of the world, that we should be holy and blameless before him (the Father). In love he (the Father) predestined us for adoption as sons through Jesus Christ, according to the purpose of his will...." Before the foundation of the world he saw and chose his children in Christ for adoption. He is intimately involved with his children and is even called El Roi, the God who sees, in Genesis 16:13.

My children enjoy being seen and acknowledged— especially in the early years. Daniel will display an especially good drawing of a dinosaur, and his younger siblings will typically call Dad upstairs to see their latest Lego© creations. But more than just looking at my kids' artwork and making sure that their shirts are not inside out (again), I need to really *see* my children. I must know their likes and dislikes, get an understanding of their desires, be aware of how to best comfort them when they are distressed, and make plans for them based on their needs.

Seeing your children in this way often becomes more complex when they are autistic. The typical verbal expressions of their emotional state and what they truly need are often not there. Therefore, more investigation, typically via the trial and error method, is necessary. I really had no clue that having Daniel hold the vacuum would help, but I had to try something. The process of trying gave me more insight into how he worked, and it gave me a course of action to take when the offending monster was the barking dog.

In Ephesians 1:7 (ESV) we see the Father sacrifice for his children: "In him (Christ) we have redemption through his (Christ's) blood, the forgiveness of our trespasses, according to the riches of his (the Father's) grace,...." Typically, when we think of the incarnation we primarily think of the sacrifice of Christ. He gave up his glory, power, and ultimately his life, to save sinners. However, when Jesus quoted the most famous verse on the planet, He did not speak of the sacrifice of the Son, but of the sacrifice of the Father. In John 3:16, it is the Father who gives. Forgiveness and grace have a cost. The penalty of sin must be paid either by the one who commits the sin or by a substitute. When the Old Testament saints wanted their sins forgiven, they sacrificed their own animals. Animals that were either loved or a potential meal were given up so that the family could have a good standing before God. But when the Father sought to have the sins of all of his children truly be forgiven, he did not ask those who sinned to sacrifice something precious to them. The one who was maligned, sacrificed that which was most precious to him, his Son. The Father's lavish gift of grace to His children could only come through lavish sacrifice.

In the attempt to be a father like the Father, I have become well acquainted with sacrifice. In early childhood, the sacrifice was time with my wife. I needed her, but the kids needed her more. After the diagnoses, the sacrifices were time and money for doctor and therapy visits. Depending on where your children are on the spectrum, certain dreams must also be sacrificed. The typical desire of fathers for their son to have that great job, a beautiful wife, and to bring home the grandkids on Christmas, may have to be replaced with the hope that one day he may be able to vacuum the house on his own. Of course, the sacrifices continue, but considering the Father's sacrifices, they are nothing, and as they bring benefit to the children that I love, again they are nothing.

The purpose of sacrificing for our children is to ensure that they have what they need. God demonstrates this in Ephesians 1:3 (ESV) as we see him serving his children: "Blessed be the God and Father of our Lord Jesus Christ, who has blessed us in Christ with every spiritual blessing in the heavenly places...." God loves His children and gives them the best that he can afford, and being God, He can afford the best of everything. Therefore, he gives us the best of everything. There is nothing that we need to live godly and fruitful lives in this world that the Father has not already given to us in Christ. In Christ, the Father gives us justification, sanctification (and with that the fruit of the Spirit), comfort, wisdom, hope, and eventually glorification.

I find it noteworthy that the gifts that God sacrificed to give us are spiritual and not physical. It is not that the physical gifts are not valuable, but they are secondary as they are of highly limited duration. I enjoy serving Daniel with things that he loves. Dinosaurs, Legos, and paper and pencils make his face light up. But like the Father, I desire to give him gifts that will last a lifetime and beyond. I want to help him overcome his fears, I want him to be able to enjoy an embrace and know that he is loved, and I want him to understand the Father's sacrifice of Christ for him, so I try to explain it in a way that he can apprehend.

There is much that we want our children to understand. Daniel is not only sensitive to sounds, but he is also insensitive to dangers around him. At church or at a friend's home the question is often asked, "Where's Daniel?" Then, the search would commence. For a while, nothing else matters as we hunt for a boy who does not recognize that it is unsafe to not be close to his parents.

The Father, too, has things he wants us to know, so he schools his children. Ephesians 1:4, 9 (ESV) points out the following: "…he (The Father) chose us in him (Christ)…that we should be holy and blameless before him (the Father)…making known to us the mystery of his (the Father's) will, according to his (the Father's) purpose, which he (the Father) set forth in Christ…" The Father's goal in educating his children is not primarily that we might become conversant with the facts and figures of the physical world, but that we reflect the character of Christ and know him by knowing Christ and by having knowledge of his plan and his will. He wants us to know that safety is found in being where he is and becoming like him. Understanding this, we recognize that the Father does not try to get back at his children for the sins they have committed (he does not punish them). Instead, he corrects his children for their own good and safety. He disciplines them.

Consequently, I don't want to just modify Daniel's behaviors so that I won't be embarrassed in public, I want to train him to make choices that will ensure his continued safety. It is true that getting agitated by sounds in public can make for an embarrassing moment, but as he gets older it could potentially make for a life-threatening encounter.

Our Father fathers us as we endeavor to father our children. Fortunately, he recognizes that in our fathering we will both make mistakes and just outright sin. As a good Father to us, he promises that if we confess our sins, he is faithful and just to forgive us our sins and to cleanse us from all unrighteousness. That is an assurance that we need. Our Father is neither passive nor abusive, and as we cling to him, he can teach us to be fathers that more closely reflect his heart.

Discussion Questions:

1. Does considering God as Father affect you positively or negatively? If negatively, what do you need to do to change your faulty reaction?

2. As a father, are there some mistakes that you have made that you find hard to forgive? How does or should your Father's willingness to forgive you affect that?

3. When you consider seeing, sacrificing for, serving and schooling your children, where do you shine? Where do you mostly fall short? How can you make gains in that area?

Parties Ain't What They Used to Be

DEBORAH ABBS

Whatever happens, conduct yourselves in a manner worthy of the gospel of Christ.

Philippians 1:27a, NIV

I used to love parties. As an extrovert, I enjoy hanging out with family and friends. Chatting, playing games, eating—what's not to love? Some might even say that formerly I was the life of the party. (Well, at least my mom said that! But, of course she's slightly biased.)

Now? Not so much.

Recently, my wonderful sister-in-law, Kim, invited us over to celebrate my niece and nephew's birthday (they are twins). Before Luke's autism diagnosis and all the issues that go along with that I would have thought, *Yay! Fun!* Now I immediately wonder, *Will Luke be in a good enough mood to go?* Or if we do go, *Will I be able to talk to anyone, or will I be chasing after Luke the whole time?*

Because of Luke's autism, he's always on the go, and large gatherings are difficult for him. Either my husband Mike or I must stick close by Luke to make sure he stays safe because he is a moving target. We have to watch him to make sure he doesn't grab someone else's food or drink because he is all about good food, just like his older brother and his mama. To make sure he

111

keeps his clothes on because being naked and free is so much more fun. To make sure all the commotion doesn't overwhelm him because he could have a meltdown. And if a dreaded meltdown occurs, it's pretty much time to head home.

For example, Mike had to work on the day of the party (a cop's work schedule often interferes with parties), so he wouldn't be there to trade off watching Luke. Sometimes Luke does great for a couple hours, but he still needs constant supervision, and I can never fully relax or let down my guard.

I often wonder why we even bother leaving the house. This gets especially difficult for us during the Thanksgiving and Christmas season. The rest of us love that time of year. Luke? Not so much. For him, the everyday routine is much better.

Here's the thing though. My older son, Brandon, loves parties. He loves hanging out with cousins and friends, and he's all about the party food, as I mentioned earlier: "What do you think they'll be serving mom?" He's a good, helpful, big brother to Luke, but I feel guilty sometimes for how different his life is because of Luke's autism. So for him alone, if nothing else, we give it a go. Thankfully, for this upcoming shindig that Kim is throwing, Mike's other brother and family live close to us and will be in attendance, so if Luke and I need to make a fast exit from the party, Brandon can stay to enjoy himself and catch a ride home with them.

Typically, when Mike is along we drive two separate cars to get-togethers so that one of us can stay longer with Brandon if Luke needs to get home. Always driving two vehicles has been a tough one for my husband, who is very conscious of fuel costs and wear and tear on the car. But that's just one of the many things we do to try and make our life work, or at least make it work a tiny bit better.

I'm glad Brandon can stay and enjoy whatever gathering we are invited to. He has a tough road sometimes. He handles it with much more patience and grace than I would have if I had a special needs sibling. Having Brandon helps challenge my impulse to circle the wagons and withdraw from the world.

Sometimes my own inner child rears its ugly head. When Mike is the one to stay longer, and I leave earlier with Luke, I complain, "What about ME?" I've certainly driven home crying from more than one social event. And even when I'm the one who stays, I miss Mike and Luke, so it never quite feels right.

Get a sitter, you might say? Yes, great idea, but someone isn't always available or qualified to do the job. Both my parents and Mike's folks are awesome and used to babysit regularly when I worked more hours for InterVarsity Christian Fellowship. As Luke's needs and issues have increased, I worry about leaving the grandparents to watch Luke for more than an hour or two, at most. When he's happy and affectionate all systems are go and his smile can light up the whole block, but his mood can change in an instant, and with it, his behavior becomes aggressive.

Something that has really helped us is having close friends who also have special needs children—of all age ranges from young kids into adulthood. We met the Clark family at Joni and Friends Family Camp a few years back, and they have become dear friends. They have three children; two of them have a disorder called Angelman Syndrome. Although different from autism, it presents very similarly, at least compared to our Lukey-boy. I'm amazed at how well their mom, Amy, takes care of her boys. It helps me when I'm overwhelmed with Luke's needs to think, *Hey, if she can do it, so can I!* and *We are not the only special needs family out there.* Plus, when we visit their house, we can let our guard down because we know she understands.

It is also helpful to have people come to our house. That way, if Luke's senses get overwhelmed, he can go to his room, rock in his bed (something he does to sooth himself), and start feeling better. We so appreciate how many of our friends and family are flexible and willing to come to us, even though I'm sure they would often prefer if we would make the drive to their place.

It's been a blessing as well to see our family and friends develop a special relationship with Luke. Many have said that Luke has taught them life lessons, and it's been fun to see some neat relationships develop. I've especially been touched to see how our friend, Mark, a big teddy bear of a guy, has treated Luke and how in return Luke loves him. Mark treats him like any other kid with his "Hey, man, how's it going, Luke? Can I get a high five?" and he often gets a huge grin from Luke in return. Another person Luke always has a smile and often a hug for when he comes over is his great-uncle, Lorin. My uncle has joy in his voice when he greets Luke with a "How's my Lukey doing today?" Lorin is an unassuming, humble guy so that might be why Luke feels so comfortable around him.

Luke is teaching me to *chill out* about parties and about having people over. I used to stress out Mike and Brandon (I don't think Luke cared), as well as myself, because I felt like the house had to be *spotless* before anyone visited. Don't get me wrong. I still clean beforehand, but I also know that Luke will be very busy before folks arrive, and there is not much I can do about it. He will be living life, getting crumbs on the floor, pulling out toys and leaving them everywhere, and generally wreaking havoc.

With so many issues involving larger gatherings, it forces me to remember Paul's words in Philippians when he says, "Whatever happens, conduct yourselves in a manner worthy of the gospel of Christ." It also helps that I have this verse tacked up on the bathroom mirror! God has also shown me, through Luke's example, what it looks like to be content with small gifts when the parties involved are celebrating a birthday or Christmas, Jesus' birthday. He is so thoroughly happy with beads, curly ribbons, and a couple of his favorite snacks. That's it. He teaches our family how to have joy in the little things and how not to be materialistic.

While it ain't no joy ride living with autism, it forces us to confront our selfishness, polish off our problem-solving skills, and appreciate even the smallest victories, like when Luke does well at a party so we can all stay for a while.

Discussion Questions:

1. Can you relate to the mixed feelings the author has about attending parties? If so how?

2. The author shares that her neurotypical son motivates her to do things instead of hiding at home and not trying. What things motivate you to keep trying and get out to gatherings or community events?

3. What special relationships has God brought into the life of your special needs child?

The God of All Comfort

MICHELE BOVELL

Blessed be the God and Father of our Lord Jesus Christ, the Father of
mercies and God of all comfort, who comforts us in all our affliction, so that
we may be able to comfort those who are in any affliction, with the comfort
with which we ourselves are comforted by God. For as we share abundantly
in Christ's sufferings, so through Christ we share abundantly in comfort too.
2 Corinthians 1:3-5, ESV

She was not who I expected to see descend the city bus steps. I
had anticipated that she would match me in size. (How else could
she have managed this child all these years?) Instead, she looked
small, frail, and enervated, as she held her son by the forearm and
crossed the Palisadoes to meet us at the hotel gate. Evelyn and I
had spoken by phone long distance several times before our
meeting. From our first conversation, I knew this would be a
learning experience for us both. Her dialect was thicker than I had
ever heard in all my years growing up on the island, and I
struggled to understand much of what she wanted to
communicate. We were from two different worlds—she, poor
with limited education, and living in a country that devalued the
weak; I, comparatively well off, with the wherewithal to locate
resources and advocate for my children. Rarely would our paths
have crossed. But as we stood in the July sun, face-to-face,
mother-to-mother, I found that we were the same, except she was
stronger and braver than I had ever had to be.

Evelyn and Earl were in their early fifties when I met them. She and her man had been together some 15 years but had never married. There was a dignity of manner about her that suggested she had been raised in a good home, and that the situation in which she now found herself was far from her dreams, or those that had been dreamed for her as a child. Earl was a good man, she would remind me. He hustled all day long for every penny, and they survived hand to mouth. Together with their son, they lived in a small board and zinc roof house, with no address, on captured land, above my childhood community. The squatters were considered pariahs, and their shantytown, a blight against what was for decades the beautiful backdrop of virgin hills. So, when one among them brought her child, so severely needy and challenged, into the local community for help, she found little.

Kurtis was Evelyn's only child, born to her later in life. When Kurtis was two years old, a pediatrician recognized his symptoms and referred him to be evaluated. A specialist confirmed the diagnosis of autism but did not tell his mother what it meant or how to address his needs. Jamaica has free healthcare, but in this developing country, therapies and early interventions are reserved for those who can afford it. Eventually, when he came of age to attend school, he was placed in the special education unit of the local elementary school. There, too, he fell through the cracks, left in the care of a quick turnover of inadequately trained teachers and aides. The few hours of separation from her son each day were no respite for her. Neighbors would come with the news that her son, with the mental capacity of a toddler, had wandered from school, and was near the edge of the busy highway. She would have to run the mile to rescue him, past the school and its teachers, who were oblivious to his absence.

By the time he came into my life, Kurtis was nine years old. He was nonverbal, hyperactive, and highly sensitive to certain stimuli. He had little ability to communicate. Evelyn told me that she had learned of the PECs system from a single visit to a speech pathologist, but that he had been denied the materials because she could not afford the $600 fee (the equivalent of $7 USD). She did her best at home and sent him to the only institution open to him. Without adequate treatment, however, his behavior became difficult to manage, and his teachers insisted that he be heavily medicated to attend the program. For certain, that meant no more escaping, but it also meant that he was completely disengaged from his peers and that he could not participate in or gain value from classroom activities.

This is the Kurtis that I met in 2007, and through him, his mother, Evelyn. I have only seen them face-to-face a handful of times. For the most part, we have had a phone relationship. Given international rates, our communication has had to be concise and purposeful. But beyond our discussions of Kurtis' physical and therapeutic needs, I've always tried to give some space to just be present with her. She's needed that—some time where I wouldn't give advice but would just offer the listening ear of a friend: *He's using scissors well; he's helping me carry things; he's repeating words heard on the television.* I've needed those times, too, for my friendship with Evelyn has put my own experiences into perspective.

Each year of Kurtis' life, Evelyn has given up a little more of herself to care for and protect her boy so that he could achieve some small developmental gain. Caring for her son, with little support, has required all her energy. It shows in her wearied eyes and inflamed joints. Coming from America, where even at our greatest points of suffering we strive to give the illusion of strength and control, I was taken aback by her meekness in that first meeting. And so, I felt a little self-conscious standing there in full makeup and jewels.

I was immediately confronted with what it was that I needed to communicate to this mother. Was I coming as savior with my money and knowledge? Certainly, God would use those, and my husband and I felt compelled to give sacrificially. But these had not proven to be our family's salvation. And so, from our first meeting that summer, we sought to stress that we were merely conduits of God's intervention in their lives: The Lord had seen Kurtis' need and was providing physical aid and emotional support through us, but his greater gift to them was himself. I'm grateful that the Lord set our own hearts straight very early on about why we were serving this family. We were not the heroes, we were not their hope, and so with physical gifts came gospel truth: God had sought them out in their sin, in their brokenness, and in their despair. He, himself, is the "Father of mercies and the God of all comfort". The comfort came in the form of physical relief, in our friendship, and in Christian love, but mercy came in the proclamation of the hope of the cross and the Father's forgiveness. In receiving the comfort, and recognizing it as a gift from God, they became open to receiving the "Father of mercies"; and as I recount in *The Gift of Empathy*, after several years of investing in their family, Evelyn and Earl would come to saving faith in Christ.

I have been watching my friends move each year from fear and anxiety over legitimate needs and concerns to a place of greater rest. Kurtis is in a safer and more appropriate school environment, but now, a young adult, he is still nonverbal and completely dependent on caregivers. I hope to assume his care one day, but his future is uncertain. Evelyn and Earl continue to struggle financially, and though they would like to move from the hardship of life in the hills, they know Kurtis is safer there than in the city streets. Evelyn's health is deteriorating rapidly, as arthritis ravages her joints. Yet, in the midst of this, there is comfort, and evidence that though their outer selves are wasting away, their inner selves are being renewed day by day.

Discussion Questions:

1. How has the Lord proven himself both the Father of mercy and the God of all comfort in your experience of caring for a loved one on the spectrum?

2. What can it mean practically in your life to "comfort…with the comfort with which we ourselves are comforted by God"?

3. How can extending ourselves to others in need deepen our own experience of the Lord's comfort?

Make Lattes, Not War

KELLI RA ANDERSON

Then Peter came and said to Him, "Lord, how often shall my brother sin against me and I forgive him? Up to seven times?" Jesus said to him, "I do not say to you, up to seven times, but up to seventy times seven."
Matthew 18:21-22, NASB

Forgiveness. It seems like a 1,000-pound bench press, a crushing load, impossibly heavy to lift. But forgiveness isn't a one-time heft above our heads to declare our spiritual duty done. It's more like a marathon. (Or, for those like me, who shudder at the thought of running a 5K, more like a *really* long-distance stroll, preferably with a comforting coffee in hand.)

But whether you resonate with a 5K run or a latte-sipping walk, in the world of special needs parenting, forgiveness is a journey we are compelled to take far too often.

I first learned about the hard discipline of forgiveness and the endurance it requires twenty-five years ago. For reasons no one has ever quite understood, my parents walked out of my life and away from their extended families, as well, severing ties from their own parents, brothers and sisters, never to contact any of us again.

The last time I saw them was August 18, 1990, my wedding day. Nearing the end of our reception, guests beginning to depart, my father approached me and took me aside. I was still

123

in my wedding gown (finally, blissfully barefoot beneath billows of white taffeta) and anxious to wave a final goodbye to family and friends from behind the wheel of my husband's gold "vet" (a 1984 Chevette).

But my father's face was stern. His jaw muscles tensed with anger, as he told me he and my mother thought I had made a big mistake. His baritone voice cracked mid-sentence, revealing a wound of bitter resolve. He cleared his throat, but said no more, and walked away.

The process it takes to grieve and to give our hurts to God takes time. It can even take years. Especially when efforts to reconcile end in failure. There were so many times when something would trigger my memories anew, and the anger I thought I had defeated would rise again to the surface, along with the tears.

But with each resurrection of old feelings, I knew the path to continued healing was to give my pain and my parents back to God and to remember that they were His responsibility. Only He could work in their lives. Only He could understand them and love them and turn their hearts toward Him. So I began to pray for God's mercy toward them and for their healing. Eventually, God turned my hurt into compassion, and forgiveness has turned pain into peace even though our relationship remains broken.

But as a special needs parent, many other people and circumstances have provided new opportunities to wrestle with the forgiveness process. And sometimes, it is a battle I don't always realize I am fighting.

One morning as I prayed in my usual, audible way through the Lord's Prayer, paraphrasing each section to make it my own, I came to the familiar line, "Forgive me my sins, as I forgive those who sin against me." I paused, expecting the usual empty thoughts to assure me that all was well in this particular department. Instead, images came to mind of several people from my son's school. God had placed His physician's hand over my heart, and I winced from the pain that was festering there.

We had had a difficult beginning to the school year. Despite our effort to intervene early to ensure a smooth transition, many mistakes were made with my son's registration and important aspects of his IEP ignored or neglected by those who knew better. Mistakes that have felt like betrayal. Mistakes that led to needless anxiety attacks, needless meetings, and lasting results that cannot be undone. It has been maddening.

As special needs parents, we are often at the mercy of teachers, administrators, doctors, and other professionals. We want their understanding and need their insights and cooperation as we try to help our children navigate this life.

At times we are blessed by those who care for our children and help us on our way. But what happens when someone harms our child? When they do not choose to do their job? Or we wrestle with an institution whose rules and guidelines are outdated and inflexible? What are we to do? How are we to respond?

Whole books are written to answer that question. And people answer it in different ways, depending on their circumstances. But as believers in Christ, whether we roll up our sleeves and attempt to correct the injustice or decide to change course and look for a better source of help, we are all called to respond with the attitude of Christ. (One reason I thank God repeatedly for the invention of the delete button to rewrite my thoughts until my digital rants are transformed into a more Christ-like tone.)

We are also called to forgive. Jesus calls us from his example on the cross to reject the toxic heart-decay of bitterness, to relinquish our desire for revenge, and to entrust to God's judgment and His care, those who have caused harm. Those who even sin against our children.

Our school battle is still unresolved. We are unsure which way we will turn. Will we patiently forge a new path for our son despite the resistance of rules and rule-keepers who seem so intent on doing the least for the "least of these"? Will we bring in an advocate to help change the system? Or will we walk away to search for another educational alternative?

No matter the choice God will help us to make, one thing remains constant. I need to forgive those who hurt and anger us, regardless of whether they change, apologize, or understand our position. And not because what they have done is excusable. It isn't. But because God's grace forgives me when I am inexcusable, grace that in turn sets me free to forgive. But what does that look like when my emotions are in such turmoil?

In Matthew 18:21-22, Peter asked Jesus if he should forgive seven times (a number above and beyond what was required by the law). Jesus corrected his dear friend saying not seven times, but seventy times seven. Forgiveness has no limits. We must forgive *as many times as it takes* to set our hearts free from anger's deadly toxins.

Right now, in the middle of my family's current mess, I will tell you, it is hard. I keep envisioning revenge scenarios that would make Dirty Harry proud. And each time, when I finally realize what I'm doing, God reminds me to stop. To remember. To confess. And to pray. *As many times as it takes.*

Seventy times seven.

So today I choose to pray by name for those whose actions are causing so much stress. And I choose to give thanks to God, not knowing what He will do, but knowing that he will work all these things together for His good purposes.

Maybe it will only take me seven times to forgive this time. But it is more likely it will take much more. Bottom line? I am going to need a few lattes for this journey.

Discussion Questions:

1. Is there a person you need to forgive so that God can release you from the toxic grip of bitterness?

2. Do you have a victory story of how God has enabled you to forgive and set you free to pray for those who may have caused harm in your family?

3. Is there someone who can pray for you and with you that God will give you the grace to forgive and be free?

Structure: Support or Straightjacket?

KEVIN O'BRIEN

To humans belong the plans of the heart,
but from the Lord comes the proper answer of the tongue.
All a person's ways seem pure to them,
but motives are weighed by the Lord.
Commit to the Lord whatever you do,
and he will establish your plans.
The Lord works out everything to its proper end...

Proverbs 16:1-4a, NIV

Every parent of an autistic child knows the value of routine. Value. Maybe we could replace that word. Necessity? Demands? "The complete and total master of everything that happens in life also known as"? All are true. Routine is the double-edged sword of the lives that we lead.

Support or straightjacket?

Well, I guess that all depends. Am I trying to get him off to school or to be flexible enough so that we can be out past nine? In the first instance, definitely support. In the second, not so much.

My wife and I are pretty much laid-back people. We go with the flow, taking things as they come. Structure has never been one of our strong suits. I wouldn't call us flighty or unable to deal with structure, just not motivated by it.

129

Nate is an entirely different story. His clock has started to rule his life. Routine has been important to him for some time. The school year provides structure and comfort. It eases his mind. Makes him feel comfortable. There is a timetable for waking up and getting the day started. Lunch is predictable. So are the subjects that he studies and his return trip home.

By the time that the end of July rolls around, Nate needs school back. (So does Loretta, truth be told.) Unbelievably, the freedom of the summer months takes its toll on his mental state. He gets agitated easily, out of sorts and crabby. It's amazing what happens when we get past the first week or so of school. The routine settles in and stress levels go down.

This is not to say that he never needs a break, of course. We all do, and Nate is no different. But Nate needs planned breaks from his routine. Breaks that he can predict, like Winter Break. Spontaneity is not exactly in his wheelhouse.

School routines are most certainly a support for Nathan. They are a support for all of us, really. In the back of my mind I find myself asking/not asking the terrifying question: "What will happen when school is done and that routine goes away?" It's a significant question.

Nathan's need for structure goes well beyond the need for school routines though. It has morphed and evolved over time. It's everywhere. Like the roots of a particularly invasive weed, it spreads and suddenly there are little shoots everywhere.

A few years ago Nate got an alarm clock. I don't remember when exactly. We thought it would be a good thing. He had started to really pay attention to the clock. And we thought that this would be helpful for him. Now we aren't so sure. We have given serious thought to removing the thing. Support has become a straightjacket.

Nate's alarm is set for 7 a.m. He gets up every day at that time, feeds the dog and starts his day. He has set his own time for bed—9 p.m. Generally that's a good thing. How many parents would kill not to have to battle kids into bed every night, especially on school nights? We don't have to tell him to get PJs on, to brush his teeth, none of it. However (there had to be one right?), all is not peaceful in the O'Brien kingdom. On Friday nights our small group meets at our house. The kids go downstairs so that the adults can have our study and pray and, well, be adults together. It's a theory anyway. Around 8:30 or so, we start to hear the pounding of feet on the stairs, the door opens and Nate checks the clock on the stove to make sure that he isn't late. This repeats itself four, five times or more. He simply cannot go past 9, and that's the easy one. Ever tried keeping a rigid bedtime schedule on vacation, how about going out for the evening and coming home after nine? Doesn't work. We've resorted to bribery to get our kid to stay up later on vacation and have all but given up on being out past nine without grandma watching him—at our house. What kind of kid DOESN'T want to stay up later? I alternate between laughing and tearing my hair out in frustration.

But schedules go beyond just the clock.

Nate is aware of the milestones of life, things like graduations and birthdays and changes in status. When he "graduated" from fifth grade, Nate realized something that we hadn't thought of.

Youth Group.

Almost immediately we heard the simple question, "When will I be a newcomer in youth group?" He was now a middle school student and that means youth group. He was VERY aware of it.

Have you ever been to a junior high youth group meeting? Maybe you went to them, maybe you didn't, but chances are, if you are like most people, remembering junior high is not exactly on the top of your priority list. Junior high youth group is barely controlled chaos that is teetering on the edge of total lack of control at any second. It's like herding cats, but a lot less fuzzy. The truth of the matter is that Nate would never survive going to youth group week in and week out. He can't handle the chaos. He really doesn't want to do the things that are a part of youth group. I think youth group and see instant meltdown and embarrassing behavior for his older brother to deal with. The need for someone with him at all times. It took a while to get past his need to be a part of youth group. It opened my eyes to just how far the need for structure goes with Nathan.

It started to dawn on us, for Nate structure extends way beyond the day to day. It's everywhere. He has plans for high school and college and marriage and career and, yes, even retirement (I wish I had it that together as a thirteen-year-old. He has mentally organized the world into these categories. These are the things that you do at certain stages in life.

It's easy for life to get out of whack. For some of us, it's easy to give up on planning, let life happen and simply react. For others, the opposite is true. We thrive on task lists and schedules and plan, plan, plan. (For the record, I am not in the latter camp naturally.) Having a child with autism is going to throw a monkey wrench into our lives no matter which way we lean. Nate's need for structure and routine has helped me to examine its place in my life.

132

I am learning that I need to be a better planner in life largely because of my son. Nate may be over the top in his need for structure, but it's a matter of degree, something to be managed, not denied. Nate's self-discipline when it comes to following an established schedule is nothing short of amazing. My days would be far more productive if I had that kind of discipline. It is something that I need.

Proverbs 16 tells us that it is in our nature to plan (*v. 1*). I think the implication is that plans aren't a bad thing at all. We make plans by the things that motivate us, the things that we value (*v. 2*). Even an autistic kid like Nate does this. He values routine. He values the certain stages in life, and so he plans around them.

But our plans are not the end either. I have also learned that part of life is adjusting our plans to the needs of others. Nate has a hard time doing that, and it can create havoc. Perhaps the hardest thing for me is knowing my plan is better than what Nate has in mind. Knowing that he can't see what I see, but that if he did, he would want what I want for him.

This, of course, is the flip side of Proverbs 16:1-4. We can and do plan according to our own needs and desires, but there is a danger here. We have all had our plans go awry. How many of us expected to have a child on the spectrum? But here we are living on it. The book of Proverbs is not a magic bullet for a perfect life. Its wisdom is in helping us to orient our lives properly.

When we make ourselves—or even our autistic children— the center of our planning, one thing is certain. The support that we need will become a self- inflicted straightjacket. It is only when we realize that our plans must be centered not on ourselves but on God that they can truly be the support that we need. Our plans will fail us. Circumstances will change. Life will happen. And we will need to adjust. When our plans are centered on God and not ourselves our perspective begins to change. My tendency is to create a plan and then ask God to bless it. I'm dedicating it to him, right? Of course this misses the point of verse three entirely. We need to center our planning on the things that God has shown us about who He is and what He is doing in the world. It is when we do this, when we center our plans on Him, that we will have plans that will be established by Him.

Proverbs 16:4a reminds us that God is in control, no matter what happens in our lives or those of our children. This fact should not lead us to abandon planning, but rather to remember that God has planned everything for His own purposes. He is the original planner. He can and does take even our messed up lives and struggles and make something beautiful from them.

Discussion Questions:

1. Do you like or avoid planning? Why?

2. What is the hardest thing for you to face with respect to your child's need for structure?

3. Are you willing to give your desires and plans, even the ones for your child over to God? Why or why not?

Why Can't We Be Friends?

BARBARA K. DITTRICH

That's how it is with us. There are many of us, but we each are part of the body of Christ, as well as part of one another.

Romans 12:5, CEV

Is there anything more heartbreaking for parents than watching our children on the spectrum struggle for acceptance and friendship?

What other parents take for granted painfully eludes us. Depending upon where a child falls on the spectrum, apraxia of speech may create a huge obstacle in relationships. Our children's behaviors may repeatedly create the experience of being invited to a play date, never to be invited again. "Quirkiness" or oddities may be overlooked by another child initially, but later drive that same child away. Or if diagnosing of a child takes years, as it did for our family, judgment and ostracizing can flow freely from other parents who just don't understand.

Our journey down the path to friendship has been a long, painful one. Having moved into a new subdivision just a year prior to our youngest daughter's birth, it was only natural for us to quickly build friendships with all the growing families up and down our block. In fact, one neighbor and I had our youngest girls only two months apart, so it was only natural to bring them together as friends when they were toddlers.

As the children grew, the differences in our daughter began to become noticeable. Heavy judgment and disdain first came from adults. Neighbors began to treat our girl as if she were naughty and problematic to have around. I was treated as if I were a negligent parent, not giving enough attention and discipline to my child. One of my siblings joined in, mocking her behind our back along with his spouse, implying that we didn't have control of our children like good parents should. Suddenly, we weren't invited to neighborhood activities any more. Family gatherings became strained, as unrealistic expectations of our daughter brought out inappropriate correction or defensiveness from others. Our isolation grew.

Difficulty with other children almost immediately followed. The boy next door decided he didn't like our affected daughter and made it his mission to spew his toxicity towards her in any and every way he could. After his parents suddenly decided to put invasive bushes along our shared property line, he would jeer at her through the young saplings. He even accused her of cutting one of the bushes at some point, which landed his enraged, irrational father at our front door. Never mind that there are rabbits feasting aplenty in our yards, and there was no witness to this crime! It was assumed that I was a negligent parent, so it was obvious that my evil daughter had been sitting there with scissors, chopping at their bushes without my knowledge. Shortly after, I caught their son once again hissing at our girl through the hedge, and I told him that I would gladly ring his doorbell to tell his mother what he was doing. That finally brought an end to his taunts through the foliage.

Unwilling to let our daughter remain ostracized and friendless, we began to pursue activities in which she had an interest. Of course, her diagnoses made her different from the typical girl. Still, we embraced her personality, pouring love on her and delighting in who God uniquely created her to be. This initially involved enrolling her in a summer T-ball program. She was one of two girls on the team and had a wonderful experience. That fall, we enrolled her as the only girl in her flag football league. She grew immensely from that experience. The parents and children welcomed us with open arms. We all hated to see that season end.

As school progressed, our daughter began finding far more acceptance from boys than from her female peers. Her ADHD attracted her to much more physical activities than the other girls her age. Running, kicking, and tossing a ball made soccer and football her favorite recess activities. Her sensory processing disorder also had her wearing much more gender neutral or boy clothes, so while her female classmates began to gossip and ridicule, her male friends just seemed to accept her as "one of the guys".

You can imagine our shock, however, when a five-year-old boy at her school told her that she could just have surgery to become a boy. Needless to say, that wasn't the type of acceptance that we wanted her to have or thought she was getting.

Lacking a diagnosis of Asperger's at this time, I wrestled deeply with what I was doing wrong. I did not encounter these same challenges with my older daughter and son. Yet, these social issues weighed heavily on us as a family. Was I allowing her to spend too much time with boys? Was I wrong to let her wear clothes that helped her with her sensory issues? Why was she so mistreated and maligned by others? What would it take for them to see the remarkable child trapped inside these behaviors and challenges?

Trying to talk her through the journey of friendships reflected our own communication hurdles at home. Her social processing issues had her vacillating between having a stiff upper lip where she showed no emotion and sobbing like a rain cloud because she was unable to verbally express what she was experiencing. It broke my heart hearing her saying things like, "I annoy everybody." or "I just wish I was normal."

Persistence, love, and solid Scriptural teaching at home were the keys to our survival. First off, we never avoided the elephant in the room regarding sexuality. We were not foolish enough to believe that others' perceptions of what was acceptable matched ours. It helped to know that she had crushes on some of these boys, and they had crushes on her, but it made me even more determined in setting boundaries around defining acceptable behavior and interaction. Encouragement came in the form of showing her successful female athletes in both professional and Olympic sports. Validating her value as a human being never waned. She needed to be filled up at home in order to go out and face a nasty, unfriendly world.

God's unfolding truth also helped encourage us as parents. While churches may still struggle to get inclusion right, there is no question about what the Bible has to say on such matters. Reading Romans 12:3-8 reveals that there is absolutely a place for each one of us, including our on the spectrum daughter. Those who would act with arrogance and alienation lack spiritual maturity and are deeply in need of prayer themselves. The behavior of others became more about them and less about us when viewed through the lens of God's Word.

While things are currently neither perfect nor easy in our daughter's life, each year she slowly improves in finding friends and engaging socially in an appropriate manner. At least one of her dearest friends faces her same challenges. She treasures the unspoken understanding and love she feels from his friendship. The vast majority of her closest friends still remain male, but she has also found other "quirky" girls like her who offer her the fun interaction she craves. Robotics, video gaming, and Tae Kwon Do have since replaced the other favorite activities she once pursued. Yet I finally see her beginning to embrace who she knows herself to be. If you are a fellow spectrum parent, I don't have to tell you what a huge step that is!

Perhaps learning to be our own best friend is the most important human friendship we can encourage our kids to pursue. There are so many frustrations and sorrows that come with being locked in a personal prison of faulty executive functioning. It is easy to see why children like our daughter can become so aggravated and self-loathing. Yet, if we as parents are the good-finders, pointing our children to their unique gifts, playing up those talents, our children are likely to eventually have that imprinted on their own minds. That appreciation of self and identification of areas of giftedness comprise parts of being our own best friend.

God loves our children, along with their remarkable uniqueness. Impressing that upon our children's hearts gives them something eternal to hold onto. When the going gets tough, there is no greater friend to have than Jesus. We need to remind them that they are a critical part of a much larger body, whether others recognize it or not. This helps build their self-esteem.

My prayer is that every one of our children, including my daughter, would learn that they are a friend worth having; and that each of these kids realize that they make this world a much richer place. Our journey down the path to friendship may be a long, painful one, but it's one worth making.

Discussion Questions:

1. What struggles has your family faced with friendships? How have you addressed those challenges?

2. Do you find it easier to let your child opt out of social activity? Why or Why not?

3. What are your thoughts on teaching your child with social deficits to become their own best friend? Do you believe that is possible? Is it a pursuit that is worth your time and energy?

4. How do you envision your child engaging socially as they reach their adult years?

The Manicure

KATHLEEN DEYER BOLDUC

Remember not the former things, nor consider the things of old. Behold, I am doing a new thing; now it springs forth, do you not perceive it? I will make a way in the wilderness and rivers in the desert.

Isaiah 43:18-19, ESV

Fifteen years ago, when my son Joel was fourteen and in the middle of a more-than-difficult adolescence, I led a workshop for parents and grandparents of children with disabilities at Ghost Ranch in Abiquiú, New Mexico. The title of the workshop was "Embracing Our Brokenness", an apt title for me, the presenter, as I struggled to come to terms with my own brokenness as the mother of a son with autism.

While at the ranch, I met Marcia, a mother whose 18-year-old son with intellectual disabilities had recently moved to a group home. Marcia was not part of my workshop—she was there for an art class—but she knew what I was teaching and sought me out as a fellow mom of a kid with special needs.

I spent several hours of my free time with Marcia that week, peppering her with questions: *How did you make the decision that it was the right time to move your son? How did you find the right place for him? How did you summon the courage to move forward? What was the transition like for him? What was it like for you?* I couldn't begin to imagine letting my baby go, but I was afraid we were going to have to do it soon.

My husband Wally and I had decided when Joel was a pre-teen that it was imperative for Joel to have the same opportunities that would be offered to his big brothers as adults—the opportunity to make his way in the world with a job, friends, and home of his own. We knew this would look different, in many ways, from his brothers' futures—it would involve supported employment rather than college or a good-paying job; it would require 24/7 support; it would have to be close to our home so that we could be involved on a weekly basis. Our goal? To find the perfect place for Joel to live when he was in his mid-twenties.

But at the time of this retreat Joel was only fourteen, and I was struggling with a growing fear that we might not be able to keep him at home for ten more years. I honestly didn't know if we'd make it through another year! His growing anxiety led to numerous daily meltdowns. Despite medications, diet changes, music therapy, occupational therapy, physical therapy, and the help of behavioral specialists, his meltdowns resulted in aggression that was becoming harder and harder for me to deal with safely.

However, I couldn't begin to imagine letting my baby go at twenty-five, much less fifteen.

Marcia and I spoke of many things over the course of that week, but one story she told resurfaces in my mind again and again.

Yes, she said, she grieved her son's transition to a group home, which was a ninety-minute drive from where the family lived. But she'd found an antidote to the grief—intimate time spent with her son during her weekly visits when she manicured his nails. There was something about the warm closeness of their bodies as they sat side by side, she said. There was an intimacy in holding his hand in hers as she clipped away the overgrown nails and filed them down to smoothness, which fed her spirit. She knew in this time with her son, she told me, that everything was okay—that life was as it should be—that this moving away from home was the normal passage of life for a young, adult son—that she was still needed as his mother, even if for this small task alone.

Her story painted a lasting picture on my heart.

We successfully made it through Joel's teen years without having to find an out-of-home placement. I thank God for that. Ten years after meeting Marcia, when Joel was twenty-four, we found the perfect home for Joel—Safe Haven Farms, a brand-new community of choice for adults with autism located just forty-five minutes from our home in southwest Ohio. While I was excited about the prospect of Joel living in a farming community, I began to grieve the transition weeks before it even happened.

Like all parents of kids with autism, we had put extraordinary time and energy into Joel, the youngest of our three sons. We loved him no more than we loved his brothers, Matt and Justin, but because of his autism, his cognitive and behavioral challenges, we had gifted Joel with so much more of our time. We knew that when he moved from our home the woven texture of our lives would be torn—a tear that would need to be patched in new ways of being with Joel—having him home for dinners, overnights, concerts, church services.

One day, before he moved to the farm, I gave Joel a manicure. We sat close together on the couch. I held his hands in mine. I clipped away the overgrown nails, white quarter-moons that fell into my lap. I admired, out loud, the strength and resiliency of his nails—so different than mine, which break and tear and crack. He smiled as I talked and clipped and filed until his hands looked fine enough for a photo shoot. I gave him a hug before scooping the clippings into my hand and walking into the kitchen to throw them into the wastebasket.

I practiced saying goodbye as I threw those clippings away—those parts of Joel that were outgrown and no longer needed—those clippings that were now a part of his past. I practiced saying goodbye as Wally and I approached the day when we would gently shove Joel over the side of the nest, whispering, "Fly, Joel! Fly!" And as I practiced saying goodbye, I reminded myself that new life would emerge—for Joel, for his father and me, for our family as a whole—new life as strong and resilient as the new nails that even at that very moment were beginning to emerge on Joel's beautiful hands.

Discussion Questions:

1. We cannot receive the gifts God has to give us when our hands are tightly clenched. Sit for a few moments in a quiet space. What do you need to let go of today? Ask God for the grace to be able to loosen your grip. Place your hands palm upward in your lap as a symbol of your desire to let go, even if you are not yet ready to do so.

2. Take some time to dream out loud, with your spouse or a friend, about your child's future. Give your imagination free rein. Don't limit yourself to what is practical or do-able. What can you see him doing as an adult? Where can you see her thriving? If this is a difficult exercise, ask God to give you new dreams and new visions for the future of everyone in your family.

3. Take some time to dream about your future with your spouse—your "empty nest" future. Pack a picnic for the park or

reserve a quiet table at your favorite restaurant. What do you see yourselves doing in ten, twenty, and thirty years? Brainstorm. Dream big. Embody your ideas by writing them down on paper. You may even want to put together a vision board, using pictures from a magazine to make your ideas visible. Pray over your list when you're finished, asking God to sift the wheat from the chaff and to empower you to reach toward those dreams that He has planted within you.

The Gift of Adversity

MICHELE BOVELL

[We] rejoice in our sufferings, knowing that suffering produces endurance, and endurance produces character, and character produces hope, and hope does not put us to shame, because God's love has been poured into our hearts through the Holy Spirit who has been given to us.

Romans 5:3-5, ESV

Sharon and I sat across from each other watching our boys solitarily preoccupied with toys on the ground. This space with Kelly green walls and murals of stylized animals had only a week earlier welcomed a dozen children to share in games and Bible choruses. But all was still now, except for the muffled sounds from the sanctuary. We didn't quite know what to say to each other; I was too embarrassed to say much. Her family had not been to church for at least a year. I had coaxed her attendance with the promise that this church was different. My husband and I had not been attending long ourselves, but when I spoke with the director, I came away confident that she had heard, and understood, and shared the vision to open a special needs classroom. I thought of not only my own son but also of all the others I was quite sure would flood in when word got out. Instead, we found ourselves in an empty classroom. The nursery ministry had moved to larger quarters and left us a room, but no ministry workers, no materials, no support.

My friend and her family did not stay at this church, and neither did we for very long. Having been in this position before with other ministries, and now wearied from pleading unsuccessfully with another church to see our need and to come alongside us, I gave up, too. Negotiating church attendance with two preschoolers on the spectrum, and their three young siblings, became too much for me. I stopped attending church altogether, for at least two years.

I felt isolated and frustrated with the people of God in those years. This and several other churches failed my family, as well as the families of several friends, but perhaps not in the manner I once believed. As I reflect with wiser eyes, I can recognize my own spiritual naiveté. I had a somewhat limited understanding of the gospel and, so, did not comprehend well God's sovereignty over all things in our lives. I misunderstood, too, the purpose of the local church, and my role as a member.

My sons, Ethan and Daniel, born 21 months apart and now entering young adulthood, were both diagnosed with disorders on the spectrum, as toddlers. In the early years of diagnoses and therapies, there was the clear sense that the Lord was near and a source of strength and wisdom to our family. In response to prayer, my husband and I witnessed tangible evidence of the Lord's grace, and we were quick to testify to God's goodness as we faced this weighty affliction. (There was the time when a number of faithful friends prayed specifically regarding our older son Ethan's unrelenting gastroesophageal reflux, and we were able to remove him from his medication the very next day.) And this is exactly what I understood autism and disability to be: a burden, perhaps an accident (Was it mine, or should we blame the vaccines?), but one the Lord would now enter and use to draw us into a place of deeper dependence upon himself. What I failed to grasp then, however, was a crucial element to the gospel: I had not come to terms with God's sovereignty over all things, including my children's disabilities. It was unimaginable to me at the time that the Lord himself could have allowed this to occur in our family for his good purposes, including for the benefit of his Body.

A fundamental flaw in my theology was the notion that sickness and suffering would be eliminated in this life if I had enough faith for my child and myself. To me, the mark of a strong believer was wholeness and prosperity. The mark of a good church was in its ability to mitigate suffering. When, in our eyes, a local congregation would fail to meet this need, we moved on. I had a shortsightedness that prevented me from understanding the trial of being a caregiver to a child with a disability as God's tool for my growth: that not only positively answered prayers were blessings, but so were his answers of no or not yet, equally designed for my good and growth. I wanted quick fixes and a moving testimony. I did get those, particularly as Ethan progressed through his own challenges quickly, but there were many more instances of protracted waiting, often without support.

Somehow, I had missed all the verses in the New Testament that make it clear that suffering in the life of the believer is a part of the sanctification process, that there is no path to maturity without it in one form or another. There's a dying so that something and Someone greater can live in and through us, and the pathway to that transformation is through adversity. Author Belden C. Lane says, "[G]race rarely comes in the shape of a gentle invitation to change. More often than not it appears in the form of an assault—something we're first tempted to flee. The spiritual life is seldom a matter of painless, uninterrupted growth." Unfortunately, that had been my misunderstanding of the Christian walk: it *was* an escape—from the penalty of sin and gradually from its practice in my life, but also from the evils of this world—a going around, but never through pain.

What such a theology did was cause me to be dishonest about my areas of weakness and struggle, not only regarding the experience of raising children with special needs, but mothering in general, my struggle with depression, postpartum OCD, hidden fears and temptations. A theology that says that the truly blessed and faithful are free from suffering set me up for chronic discontent (with myself, my spouse, the local church) and even despair, and denied me the blessing of experiencing a level of God's grace accessible only to the ones who persevere in trials. To the contrary, the freedom of later understanding that God not only ordains suffering, but is present in it with me, allowed me to embrace my lot—all of it—and so be freed to be more honest about who I am, to embrace my children more fully for the gifts they are, to depend more fully on the Lord, and to experience and testify to grace found sufficient for the need.

As I revisit those early church experiences as a mother of children on the spectrum, I'm grateful to the Lord for maturation in his Word that now allows me to see my own erroneous thinking and the limited way in which I approached my relationship with the church. There does need to be a greater effort among local churches to educate and prepare themselves to meet the needs of every person the Lord calls. But I think the greatest gift a community of believers offers those affected by disability is to engage us, week after week, with the gospel. It is to tell the truth about uncomfortable grace and the painful path to sanctification, and to proclaim the worship and magnification of God as the highest priority in the lives of their members, for worship eclipses and brings into perspective our trials.

Discussion Questions:

1. What are my assumptions about the sovereignty of God? How does my experience with autism challenge these assumptions?

2. What is my view of the grace of God? How have I seen the grace of God in my own life, and that of my loved one on the spectrum?

Big Surprise! We Are Weak

DEBORAH ABBS

*That is why, for Christ's sake, I delight in weaknesses, in insults, in
hardships, in persecution, in difficulties. For when I am weak, then I am
strong.*

2 Corinthians 12:10, NIV

Recently I took a spiritual gifts test. I've taken a few different ones
since I accepted Christ into my heart and life, and it's always been
good for me. After all, God's Word says He gives spiritual gifts to
each of His children for building up His Body and for His glory,
so it's a wise idea to know what they are and ask God to use them
for His benefit.

But have you ever taken a what-are-my-top three-
weaknesses test?

Me neither.

Doesn't sound very fun, does it? If we are honest, I'm
guessing we can each come up with our areas of weakness pretty
easily—no test required. At least, I know I can. And if for some
odd reason we can't, our families sure can remind us whether we
want them to or not!

I have an issue with my temper. Brandon, my older son,
has an issue with waking up for school in the morning. His alarm
doesn't do the trick, so I go into his room at 6:40 a.m., and I say,
"Morning, honey. Time to wake up."

Brandon, pulling the blanket off his head, mumbles inaudibly.

At 7:00 a.m., I warn him, "Brandon, get up. You have twenty minutes until you have to go."

Brandon replies while still, technically, sleeping, "Okay, I'm up."

At 7:10 a.m., I shout, "GET UP NOW! I AM NOT driving you to school if you miss the bus!"

Brandon, finally up, shouts back, "OKAY!"

It's finally 7:22 a.m. and Brandon is heading out the door (bus comes in three minutes). He says, "Wow, Mom, why do you have to be so mean?"

Okay, so in this example yelling might be appropriate, but usually when I blow my top, it is out of proportion to the issue and can be explosive. One of the many thorns in my flesh.

Paul writes in 2 Corinthians 12:7 that God gave him a thorn in the flesh to "keep [him] from becoming conceited" (NIV). We don't know specifically what this "thorn" was, but we know that he pleaded with the Lord three times to take it away. God said to Paul, in 2 Corinthians 12:9, "My grace is sufficient for you, for my power is made perfect in weakness" (NIV). Did you catch that? *God's power* is somehow made perfect in *weakness*. As God so often does, He flips things upside down and all around. After all, wouldn't it make more sense, to us at least, if God said His power was made perfect in our strength?

So it is just as surprising when Paul says in 2 Corinthians 12:10, "That is why, for Christ's sake, I delight in weaknesses, in insults, in hardships, in persecution, in difficulties. *For, when I am weak then I am strong*" (NIV, emphasis added).

154

God's strength being shown in my many weaknesses hit home for me in a very real way back when I was a college student. Before I met and started dating my husband Mike, I dated someone who wasn't a Christian. (Yes, I know, Paul also has something to say about this in 2 Corinthians 6, but that's not why I bring it up here.) My boyfriend started attending InterVarsity Christian Fellowship with me at the College of DuPage, and another friend invited him to a Bible study. And, praise God, my boyfriend accepted Christ!

Shortly after he became a Christian, I asked him if there was anything in particular about me, or that I did, that helped him on his faith journey. If I wanted puffing up (I'm sure I did!), I should *not* have asked him that. He said, "I saw that you had struggles and were weak but that you got a strength and peace from somewhere else, and I wanted that in my life too." Ouch! There it is, what Paul was talking about. For when we are weak, then we are strong. What he said sticks in my mind to this day and motivates me to show not only my strengths, but my weaknesses as well, to be real and let Christ shine through. This whole topic is tricky, and here comes an extra prickly part. What does this mean for me as a parent of someone who has autism, who is mostly nonverbal? And more, what does this mean to me also as a parent of a typical teenager who has his own flaws and struggles, like every other person on the planet? To top it off, what about my own sin and weaknesses?

Another personal thorn involves my mental health, or lack thereof, at times. "Why, God?" I asked. Why, when I was pregnant with my first child did you allow me to have a manic episode and then sink into a depression so deep that I had to be hospitalized in a psychiatric ward more than once? Why did you allow me to be so ill that I didn't recover until Brandon was six months old and I had to have electroconvulsive therapy treatment to get my brain back on track?

Even more painfully, why did you allow Luke to talk and then lose his speech? Why does he have autism and have to struggle so much? If I read the Bible and believe it is true, the more accurate question should be, why not? The Lord uses the weak things of this world to convict the strong, the folks who think they have it all together.

Don't get me wrong. I'm not saying it's wrong to plead with God and ask Him to help our children. I hate seeing Luke cry and melt down when he can't communicate to me what he needs or wants. It's terrible. I do pray for peace and help for him in communicating, for him to be content and happy, and yes, for healing. And I long for the someday in heaven when I know Luke will be able to talk my ear off and tell me all his thoughts and feelings.

But God made Luke in all his Lukey-boyness. His wonder. His love of running and jumping. His smile and laugh that light up the room. And he allows his meltdowns. His getting overwhelmed and over stimulated and needing a quiet room to calm down in. His up and down moods. All of it. So who is to say that Luke needs healing or fixing when God uses him just as he is and even more so through his weaknesses? None of us is perfect here on earth. But why assume that Luke is more in need of healing than me or any other so-called "typical people"? We all need God's healing touch. It's just that Luke's needs are more obvious and out there for the world to see.

One commentator speaks of "the divine principle of power manifested through weakness"[1]. If that's the case, it follows that we need to embrace our weaknesses, share them, and even boast about them like Paul did. God's power and strength will show through, and it is amazing. I know—for me, at least—when I'm struggling and feeling my many weaknesses, that's when I pray more and seek God's help. I rely more on Christ—and isn't that what I should always be striving to do?

Discussion Questions:

1. Do you agree with the author when she says that her son is no more in need of healing than someone without special needs? Why or why not?

2. Have you experienced a time when Christ's power was displayed through your weakness? If so, what happened?

3. Is it easy for you to share your weaknesses with others? Why or why not?

---

[1] Colin G. Cruz, "2 Corinthians", in *The New Bible Commentary: 21ˢᵗ Century edition*, ed. DA Carson, et al (Downers Grove, IL: InterVarsity Press, 1994), 1204.

Home Sweet Home

KELLI RA ANDERSON

Immediately Jesus, aware in His spirit that they were reasoning that way within themselves, said to them, "Why are you reasoning about these things in your hearts? Which is easier, to say to the paralytic, 'Your sins are forgiven'; or to say, 'Get up, and pick up your pallet and walk'? But so that you may know that the Son of Man has authority on earth to forgive sins"—He said to the paralytic, "I say to you, get up, pick up your pallet and go home."
Mark 2:8-11, NASB

The day I walked into our newly purchased home my heart sank. I stood in the open doorway, at a loss for words, as my eyes adjusted to the small, dark room in front of me. I sneezed, impulsively, my nose protesting the smell of stale, musty air. The shabby curtains, some former shade of Sears-catalogue yellow, hung in tatters to the floor over the living room's few windows, shutting out the dusty light from the autumn sunshine that happily played outside.

So this was it, the house my husband had purchased while I was on pregnancy bed rest. I knew he'd done his best, and I had even given it my reluctant blessing based on its online description. After all, it was everything we wanted: It was in a neighborhood with the best elementary school, it was close to his job, it was available in time for our closing deadline, and it was in our price range.

Apparently, we forgot to make sure it was livable.

159

Boasting 1,000 square feet, there was only so much this 1948 Ranch-style could offer our newly grown family of five. With just two bedrooms, no dining room, one bathroom so small our knees hit the tub when we sat on the toilet, and one cramped, galley kitchen sporting walls of 1950s Pepto pink, it was a sore sight for my sore eyes.

I carefully set down the baby carrier, cradling my five-day-old daughter. It gently rocked on the worn wooden floors, riddled with nails and staples that once secured a shag carpet. Sarah cooed happily, unaware that anything was amiss. Her toddling brothers, ages two and four, joined in her delight as they ran to explore the house's few empty rooms, laugh at the odd echoes from their voices, and, especially, to enjoy the enormous back yard with its single, massive, towering maple. This was not the answer to prayer I had expected from months of looking for the home of our dreams. But sixteen years later, it has become the home God knew that we needed.

I think God often works like this, giving us what we need more than what we want. In the Gospel of Mark, four men lowered their paralyzed friend down through a hole they dug in a roof to reach Jesus on a crowded afternoon. And what did He grant their friend in response to their great faith in His healing? Forgiveness for his sins.

I could be wrong, but my guess is that their intention was for their friend to receive physical healing. Jesus saw a greater need and gave them more than they could know or ask or imagine. Forgiveness of sin was a gift only God could provide. And so, to prove to those who doubted that He not only had the power to heal but to forgive sins, as well, Jesus told the man to rise, take up his mat and walk. God knew what everyone needed that day.

As I sit now in my dining room addition, vaulted ceiling above my head, and listen to the sounds of my teenage sons and daughter talking into the night hours from their bedrooms, I know that this house is not just the one we needed, but it also has become the home that we wanted.

This modest house, God's gift to our family, continues to teach us patience and humility. Just last night we cleaned out and mopped up pools of water from a clogged drain in our laundry room, just one time out of countless others. (We have the routine down to an exact science.) And my knees still hit the tub whenever I use the bathroom.

But over the years my husband and I have learned to work side by side to solder copper pipe, to hang siding, to frame new walls, to build a stone fireplace, and to create a raised veggie garden (my therapeutic outlet). Miraculously, we still have all ten digits to show for it. And we are still learning, side by side, to raise three children in the midst of autism's challenges and the growing limitations of middle age.

God knew we needed this home long before we did. He knew we would face relentless waves of medical bills that would have capsized our finances had we purchased the kind of home lenders said we could afford. He knew we needed a home strong enough to bend but not break during gale-force winds of children's emotional and physical growing pains. We needed a house that could absorb the dents and broken windows, contain its uncensored belly-laughs or frustrated screams of anger, forgive the messes, and weather the countless flooded sinks, tubs, and toilets when little boys and their sensory needs were a greater challenge than the typical "snakes and snails and puppy-dog tails" of boyhood.

God also knew we needed a neighborhood of substitute grandparents, the quiet that only comes from a dead-end street, and the magical balm of nature that visited our children in the shape of squirrels, raccoons, foxes, birds of every kind, roly-poly bugs, rabbits, and even the occasional coyote or deer.

Now, with retirement just a few years away, my husband and I talk sometimes about the home we will live in and I am hard-pressed to want much more than what we already have. Yes, I would still love a bigger kitchen and maybe architecture that doesn't scream "1950s starter home".

But will the home of our dreams boast a garden that makes my oldest son stop long enough from his video games to help me cultivate and harvest? Or a "baking station" (really, just a granite remnant atop a cabinet my husband cut to fit my 5-foot height) on which my daughter and younger son invented "David's Pizzas", and current site of my daughter's baking craze?

Will it have a front closet door that sticks when you close it, decorated with sixteen years of growth marks recorded in magic marker? Will it have a silver maple with twenty-foot-high outstretched arms that gave my children hours of tree-swing "underdogs" that sent them soaring and screaming with delight? (And humored us when we made our first clumsy batches of maple syrup shared only with our bravest friends?)

No, this was not the home I was looking for sixteen years ago, but it was the home in which our young family of five could roughhouse, learn to live with autism, and make messes. And it is still the home where we are struggling to learn life lessons like "bigger isn't always better." I think God gave us what we needed and maybe that is what we should really want. Although, I wouldn't say no if He decided I needed a bigger kitchen.

Discussion Questions:

1. How has God gifted you, your marriage or your family with something that may have seemed inadequate to your needs, only to surprise you with its better purpose?

2. What are you thankful for concerning your family's unique joys and challenges reflected in the place you call "Home Sweet Home"?

3. Home is not always sweet when it includes parenting, especially (at times) with autism. In what ways can you find peace, develop creative outlets, or recharge your batteries at home?

Created in God's Image

KEVIN O'BRIEN

So God created mankind in his own image, in the image of God he created them; male and female he created them.

Genesis 1:27, NIV

"Do everyone in our community a huge favor and MOVE!!!! VAMOOSE!!!! SCRAM!!!! Move away and get out of this type of neighborhood setting!!! Go live in a trailer in the woods or something with your wild animal kid!!! . . . Do the right thing and move or euthanize him!!!"

That's just a small sample, and that wasn't all, not by a long shot. It didn't happen to my family, but it was real, and I could sympathize.

An anonymous letter sent to the grandmother of a thirteen-year-old autistic boy. The quote above is only a small part of the rant. The author, purportedly "one pissed off mother," makes it clear that she has no use for a person like Max, the autistic boy in question. I say purportedly because there are enough exclamation points in this letter to last a junior high girl a week. By my count, this 3-paragraph gem includes 27 sentences (at least three of the one word variety), 10 question marks and 114 exclamation points—I could be wrong, my eyes tend to bug out a bit when that many are strung together.

As you can probably tell there is a not so small part of me that wants to let loose with some good old-fashioned righteous indignation. Of course, that would be perilously close to stooping to the same level.

When this happened, Nate was thirteen. My wife is from Canada, and once upon a time, before my son was born, we lived not altogether too far from Max's grandmother, so it hit even closer to home for me.

I watched the stories and the comments on Internet news sites (never a good idea if you value your sanity). I have seen comments on Facebook from family and friends expressing outrage and support. I appreciate both.

But I am finding more than anything else that my feelings are not shock, not outrage, or even dismay. I have very little capacity left for the first in any arena; I have perhaps gotten a bit anesthetized to the outrage when it comes to issues of special needs. Dismay? Well, there is certainly more of that. It's a kind of sadness that a person can be so unaware of their surroundings, so self-absorbed, that they cannot see the inherent value of another, just because that person is different.

I suppose, if reality is nothing more than the universe playing dice (time plus chance and voila, here we are!), then we might as well all be as selfish as possible because that's all there is.

Of course, I don't believe that, and chances are, neither do you. Most of us believe in some kind of meaning in the universe. There may be a great variety of ways that we talk about it, and our beliefs are not the same, but they are there. The Christian and Jewish faiths claim that not only are we created by God, we are created in the very image of God—Genesis 1:27. Without getting too technical, Genesis says that in a very real sense we are living, breathing icons of God. All of us.

Of course there's a catch. There's always a catch. The story turns in Genesis 3 (quite literally the same page in the Bible I am looking at as I write this). We screwed up. We are broken. Fallen. The image still exists, but it's marred.

And so I am not terribly surprised at the brokenness of the world. And that, more than anything else, is what I see in this oh so eloquent anonymous missive. I see evidence of a person who is broken, a person in desperate need of something much greater than herself.

When I read a letter like that, I don't just worry about Nate. I wonder sometimes about where my other children will be ten or twenty years from now. How will their brother affect who they become? Will they resent the things they endure? Will they resent Nate? Or will they thrive? Will they become more than they would have been otherwise?

None of us get to choose our families. None of us has it all together. The way I see it, every one of us is broken. Some of us are just better at hiding it than others. That means every family is broken. Every family has their stuff. Families with special needs members have extra stuff. Oh, we're not alone in that. Some families have kids with cancer. Some have parents with extreme disabilities. Lots of people have extra amounts of "stuff", whatever that might be.

I really try to remember that other families deal with a lot of things that I am unaware of. Things that may well be harder than what my family deals with. I try. I'm not always terribly successful. But I am actually less worried about myself than I am my non-autistic children.

Because I am an elder in my church, I see and hear about a whole lot more than many people do. I am party to the hurts and the fears, the loneliness and despair that many face. These are the unfortunate but oh-so-real parts of life that we do not talk about. The loneliness of the single person in a church filled with married people and families. The loss and displacement after a spouse has died. Health problems of older folks and sometimes the young as well. I see the marriages that are failing because of selfishness by one or both parties. I see the hardship caused by the loss of a job, and the very real financial disasters that average people face. Mostly in silence.

The difference between those families and mine is simple. Nate may look "normal" at first glance, but when you interact with him, you know that there is something different. Nate's issues cannot be hidden if you spend any time with him. He *can't* hide them. Most of the rest of us can. Of course, there is another difference. Those families aren't mine. Even if they are friends. Even if they are people I love and care about. There is simply a distance there that can never be completely bridged.

Loretta and I spend so much time worrying about Nate, figuring out what he means and wants, trying to control the meltdowns and the quirks, that too often the other children can suffer. It's not intentional. Not a lack of love or even desire.

Sometimes you are just tired.

Sometimes they have learned to be quiet and deal with things on their own.

Sometimes you don't know how to turn off protective parent or worried parent or, well—I'm sure you've been there.

Connor is almost fifteen as I write this. High school. It's hard enough being a teenager when everything is "normal".

Parents and siblings embarrass you on principle. And sometimes they do it on purpose (who me? Never!). What do you do when your brother can't hold a normal conversation? A brother who reacts to routine things in the same annoying way every time. All the time. When he says random things, totally out of left field things, to your friends? Every time someone meets him for the first time you have to explain. When you are shy to begin with, the embarrassment factor is magnified that much more.

Sierra has it much easier in many ways. She is four years younger and has always had a different relationship with Nate than Connor. In many ways it's a more direct one because she forced it. But I see a time coming when it won't be quite so easy. When the realities of an older brother with autism will begin to come home to roost.

But as much as I worry about how Nate affects my other children, I see signs of hope. Signs that, for all of the difficulties, having a brother like Nate is something that is making them stronger.

I remember a bedtime some years ago now. At the time Nate and Connor shared a room. It had been a particularly hard evening with Nate. Connor was in bed and I was talking to him before praying. I don't remember all of the details, but I do know the conversation went something like this.

"I'm sorry it was such a difficult night, buddy. I know that sometimes it is difficult for big brothers to deal with."

"I wish there was no such thing as autism because it's hard for parents."

If my mental math is correct, Connor wasn't even in junior high when he said that. Could he have had that kind of insight and compassion for his parents if Nate wasn't his little brother? I don't know. Maybe. Probably. But I do know that God is using his little brother to shape Connor into the person that he is supposed to be. God can redeem any situation if we let him.

Don't get me wrong; Connor has his moments. He's a teenager. And like I said, we're all broken.

Sierra looks out for Nate in big and little ways. Sometimes it's scary. She's nine going on 29 and in charge of the world. She reminds Nate what to do and when to do it all the time. Sometimes remind is a bit of a misnomer. But she does it because she is looking out for him. Trying to get him to behave appropriately and to stay on task. Yes, she gets exasperated with him. She sounds like her parents. But I can see the concern. I have heard her say to virtual strangers, "He has autism; he doesn't understand." It's a part of her reality and she looks out for her big brother.

When I look at my children, all of my children, I see both brokenness and beauty. I see a family that God wants to shape into something more than it currently is.

I truly believe that we are created in the image of God. As broken as we are it is still there. I see it in the smile of my autistic son. I see it in the way that he lights up at the simplest of pleasures, how he wants others to be well and happy. He is broken. I have no doubt of this either. I see it every day. Of course, I also see that I am broken. So are we all.

Some of us are just better at hiding our brokenness. But after the dust settles, I have to ask, "Who is more broken?" The thirteen-year-old boy from the suburbs of Toronto? My now fourteen-year-old son in suburban Chicago? Or the person who wrote that not so unbelievable letter?

Discussion Questions:

1. Are you more inclined to view your autistic child as broken or created in the image of God? Why?

2. Do you worry about how your autistic child is and will affect your other children, or do you see their influence as a blessing?

3. What can you do to help your neurotypical children understand your love for them and their importance to you?

4. How is God shaping your family to be more than it is now?

Sufficient Grace

KATHLEEN DEYER BULDOC

But he said to me, "My grace is sufficient for you, for my power is made perfect in weakness." Therefore I will boast all the more gladly about my weaknesses, so that Christ's power may rest on me.

2 Corinthians 12:9, NIV

I'm sitting on the porch of Creekside Cabin in Roan Mountain, Tennessee. A gentle spring rain is falling, and a small waterfall caused by a plugged-up gutter gushes down in the grass below my Adirondack chair. My porch-side perch overlooks a roaring, rock-filled creek. Across the creek a hill ascends at a nearly vertical pitch, rhododendron jutting over the water. The white flowers of a lone dogwood pop against the lush green backdrop.

It is chilly this morning, so I'm wrapped in a cocoon of fleece: robe, jacket, and two blankets. Sipping a cup of hot tea, I am mostly warm, except for where the breeze creeps under the blankets and tickles my bare legs.

My husband Wally and I, along with our oldest son, Matt, drove down from Ohio earlier in the week. Wally and Matt backpacked a piece of the Appalachian Trail the first two days we were here, while I hung out at the cabin. When they returned yesterday, they overflowed with tales of spring beauty on the mountain. Wally took me on a wildflower hike, not wanting me to miss the spectacular sight of the forest floor covered with a

173

blanket of white, blue, and yellow violets, red trillium, wild iris, and mayapples. Most beautiful of all was the pink lady's slipper, nodding her head under spear-like leaves of green.

Normally, this would be a piece of heaven for me and I would be soaking it all in, writing poetry, holding hands with my husband as we walk the trails, snuggling in front of a fire in the evening, chatting with Matt about the flora and fauna of the Roan, looking forward to my book when I crawl into bed. Actually, my plan for these four days was to finish the young adult novel I've been working on for the past two years.

Instead, I have been stuck on a treadmill of worry. Since our son Joel's move to Safe Haven Farms (a farm for adults with autism), he has begun cycling again. We dealt with this all through his adolescence, but it had finally subsided in his early twenties. In the midst of the cycle, which comes around every three to four weeks, he can't stop moving. Walking six to eight hours a day on the farm where he lives, his inner anxiety propels him forward, even past the dropping point. He lashes out with his hands, at anyone around him, and for the first time in his twenty-seven years, he has begun destroying property. He's taken down and broken all of the family pictures we had hung on his walls, broken his new TV, and has ripped up cards and pictures from family and friends that he's received in the mail.

My heart is breaking. How can I help my son? What should we do? I pray. I make lists. I make doctor appointments. I wait, sometimes for months, to get in to see certain doctors. I wrestle with other doctors who make me feel as if I know nothing, even though I have valuable information regarding my son that they don't have. I pray some more. I worry. I obsess. I toss and turn in the middle of the night. I am on the merry-go-round from hell.

Four words sum it up: I am a mess.

This morning, I open Macrina Wiederkehr's book, *Abide: Keeping Vigil with the Word of God*, to her meditation on 2 Corinthians 12:9: "But he (the Lord) said to me, 'My grace is sufficient for you, for my power is made perfect in weakness'" (NIV). Macrina chooses the words, "my power is made perfect in weakness" for her meditation. Four words jump off the page and speak to me.

"My grace is sufficient."

I take them into the quiet. After ten minutes, only one word remains.

"Sufficient".

I open my thesaurus. God's grace is enough. God's grace is adequate, plenty, ample, satisfactory.

As I lay in bed last night between 2 and 4 a.m., I implored God to stop the merry-go-round in my brain so that I could sleep. What to do? What doctor to see? What advice to take? What meds are helping? What meds are making matters worse? What to do about the day program? We've worked so hard to build and establish this farm—a lifelong dream for our son. Do we call it quits? Pull him out?

What to do? What to do? What to do?

Finally, in exhaustion, I spoke four words to God. I repeated them over and over, a mantra to out-shout out the never-ending questions circling in my mind.

Can't live like this. Can't live like this. Can't live like this.

This morning, on this porch in the rain overlooking a creek that never quits flowing, God speaks four words back to me:

My grace is sufficient. My grace is sufficient. My grace is sufficient.

I open my eyes and take in the beauty surrounding me. Crystal clear water flowing over ancient stone. Lush green rhododendron ready to burst into bloom. Moss growing on the trees. Birdsong.

I thank God for our son, Justin, who, while we were gone for the weekend, made the long drive out to Safe Haven Farms to pick up Joel and take him to the zoo. For the community of parents that make up Safe Haven Farms, for last night's monthly dance, and the joy those dances give Joel. For our friends, Amy and Dirk, who are taking Joel to church this weekend while we're gone. For our son, Matt, who for the first time, is enjoying Roan Mountain with us. I'm so thankful that he's moved home to Ohio from Oregon. We missed him so much the eight years he was gone. For my husband, Wally, who discovered this piece of heaven with me nearly twenty years ago and who returns with me on a regular basis.

I take a deep breath and thank God for reminding me that even though the enemy wants to rob me of joy, I can step off the merry-go-round by declaring these four simple and powerful words, a mantra to see me through the hard times:

God's grace is sufficient. God's grace is sufficient. God's grace is sufficient.

Discussion Questions:

1. Transitioning a child with autism from the family home to a home in the community is a difficult process that takes years of planning. For some of us, even the thought of our child moving away from home is enough to induce a panic attack! Even with the best of planning, the transition can be hard on everyone

involved. And yet, all of us will face this decision at some point as parents of these very special, challenging children. Take some time today to pray about your son or daughter's future, no matter their age.

2. They grow up so much more quickly than we can ever imagine. How do you envision your child's future? What feelings arise as you dream about his or her adulthood?

3. Pour your feelings out to God—out loud, silently, or in your journal—and then ask God for His vision for your child. Take some time over the next few days to simply listen to what the Holy Spirit might be whispering to you, in your dreams, in the Scriptures, and in words and lives of the people around you.

Heaven

Michael Abbs

Jesus answered, "I am the way and the truth and the life. No one comes to the Father except through me."

John 14:6, NIV

I have been thinking a lot about heaven recently.

These thoughts bring up a variety of emotions. Our first baby, albeit a furry one, was our dog, Chewie. After we got him I thought about heaven more, imagining him there. I still do sometimes, especially since he died two years ago. I have heard speculation about whether animals will be in heaven from people a lot more learned in regard to the Bible than I, and there are varying opinions. The Bible doesn't say anything about animals and heaven. We will have to wait and see on that one, but I really hope they are with us.

Since my sons have been born, I think even more about what it will be like in heaven someday with them. And with my youngest being non-verbal, it has me imagining it even more.

The Bible is clear that there is a lot to look forward to, regardless of whether animals and pets are there. Many specifics about heaven are not covered in the Bible, but that doesn't mean there aren't some absolute truths: There will be rewards (Matthew 5:12); we will get new bodies (Philippians 3:21); there will be no tears or sadness (Revelation 21:4); sadly, not everyone will be there (Matthew 7:21).

I'm not yet sure how these last two points—about there being no tears or sadness and that not everyone will be there—can both be true. Many people I love have different ideas about faith, and obviously I want to see them in heaven. But since the Bible says both things—that we must believe in Jesus' amazing grace to us on the cross to be with Him always, and that there is no sadness in heaven—I'm sure they are true. The teaching that not everyone will be there means, of course, that those who do not know Jesus will not be there. Those who know Jesus as Lord will be present.

I don't know what an existence apart from God for eternity would be like. That is an extremely difficult thought. The good thing is that there is still time. God is calling, and His gift, Jesus' sacrifice that allows for salvation, is freely available to each of us!

What does this all mean for God's children who have special needs?

I have to believe that if there is not a capacity for rejecting God's gift, there will be no separation from God, in this life or after physical death. I sometimes wonder what Luke's comfort from Jesus today feels like since he can't tell me. Does he sense Jesus with him in a special way? I know that there are times that he laughs uncontrollably, and for no reason I can locate. I wonder if he is sharing a private joke with Jesus then.

As nice as that is to imagine, this is less important to me than the eternity that is to come. Some people may be tempted to view special needs, illness, or disability as reasons to not believe in God. This issue is, of course, a small part of the bigger question of why bad things happen to good people. Again, I can't claim to have the correct or full answer. Certainly, sin entering the world through the first people and continuing in everyone since (except Jesus) to the present day is part of the answer. Satan's work is another part of the answer.

To me, though, the part of the answer that is easiest for me to understand and come to terms with is that what is important, lasting, and meaningful is not really about our time here on earth. One hundred years of life (on the high end) is nothing when eternity is considered. So it makes this time here on earth, however long that is, a training ground of sorts: The place to get to know God through Jesus in preparation of knowing Him fully later.

So these special needs are not permanent! This time on earth is short, as God makes clear through James: "What is your life? You are a mist that appears for a little while and then vanishes" (James 4:14b, NIV).

As many parents with special needs children must imagine, my thoughts of Luke being fully healed are comforting and joyous ones. Seeing him in his new body, but still clearly being my "Luke", having a LONG conversation with him, and seeing him full of peace and joy is a great vision for me. I like the idea of a line of people waiting to talk to Luke, to have conversations for which they have waited a lifetime. I see his grandparents and uncle giving him a big hug and asking him what he thinks about all kinds of things. I see his big brother, Brandon, laughing and playing with him in a whole new way without having to worry about him. I see his mom looking happier than she ever has, connecting in a new way with her boy as they walk along the beach. And I see me with Luke doing things we have not yet been able to do, like going for a run and working out together, going on a campout, listening to his jokes. I'm hopeful we might be able to do some of these things during our time here on earth, but I'm confident we will be able to do these things during God's eternal life—and maybe even Chewie can join us.

Heaven will be awesome and amazing with a new level of closeness to God, and to others. After all, I will get to talk with Jesus face to face. I just don't want any loved ones, or anyone actually, to choose to miss out on this exciting eternity, when they can, most importantly, have a conversation with Jesus, and secondly, have one with Luke.

Discussion Questions:

1. What do your visions of heaven include? Are they consistent with Scripture?

2. What can you be doing to make sure your loved ones are with you in heaven?

3. Has your thinking about heaven changed since having a loved one with autism? If so, how?

God's Varied Grace

Michele Bovell

And God is able to make all grace abound to you, so that having all
sufficiency in all things at all times, you may abound in every good work.
2 Corinthians 9:8, ESV

It is August and the air conditioning is a welcome relief from the
Georgia heat. Still, the narrow room is stifling as I sit in
consultation with the psychiatry fellow, waiting for her to get to
the point. My gaze shifts between the woman's eyes and my two-
year-old spinning wildly on the stool in the background. I am
unnerved, but she is unfazed by his behavior. This is the domain
in which she operates daily. Her face is kind and sincere, and her
voice deliberately sympathetic. We speak mother to mother. There
had been a battery of tests through which Ethan had been
distracted and unresponsive. The verdict is predictable—my son
has autism. I'm tempted to cry, but steel myself instead. After all, I
knew this would be the outcome. She hands me a folder, and I flip
through it as she continues to speak. A blue sheet of paper catches
my attention. It's a list of alternative approaches, and as I skim it,
much of what she is saying escapes me. I interrupt her to inquire
her opinion of each, but she dismisses them, disputing their
efficacy. The prognosis is poor for a child like Ethan, she prepares
me, and recommends only that I enroll my son in a day program

183

at a local institution for intensive behavior modification. But she is too late. I have been armed with hope.

Using that information sheet as a guide, my husband and I researched on the web and made phone calls. Applying what we had learned, we administered supplements, tried an elimination diet, and enrolled Ethan in home-based therapies. And we prayed. Along with wisdom came courage. Unwilling to be swerved by skeptics, we persevered. Progress came surprisingly quickly. Ethan spoke his first novel phrase within a week of eliminating milk. His hyperactivity calmed down in response to supplementation, and his gastrointestinal issues resolved through experimentation with his diet. All the while, there was an international team of faith-filled Christian friends supporting us with their prayers for our boy. "I asked my friends in Japan to pray!" I recall a Kenyan pastor sharing, to our hearts' encouragement. In response, we saw tangible evidence that the Lord was near and working on our behalf.

Within a year, Ethan went from being echolalic to asking thoughtful questions. He built friendships at his little special needs preschool and quickly became the star at circle time. To his older brother's delight, he joined in pretend play and willingly recited his character's parts as directed. His stimming lessened, as did his sensitivity to sounds and other sensory stimuli. With an end to his digestive issues, he gained weight, and his sallow complexion brightened. He was progressing along at a remarkable clip and was eager to learn. It was no surprise, then, that as the close of 2001 approached, Ethan's developmental pediatrician removed his diagnosis of classical autism and replaced it with *mixed receptive-expressive language disorder*. What a breakthrough, what a testimony!

The day was bittersweet, for in that very hour, his younger brother, Daniel, just days from his second birthday, received the diagnosis of PDD-NOS. Still, given Ethan's swift progress, there seemed compelling cause to be very hopeful. We knew the routine, and we had already begun interventions a full year earlier than we did for Ethan. More important, we believed we could anticipate how God would work in our experience with disability in response to prayer. Certainly, there was another great testimony in the works! But Daniel did not progress in the same manner as did his brother. While Ethan was relatively easy to manage, Daniel was hyperactive and defensive. He did not share his brother's poor muscle tone and gastrointestinal struggles, which meant he had a great deal more energy. He fought every attempt to hold him and to demonstrate physical affection. Seeking sensory input, he hummed loudly and banged his forehead until it bled on any firm surface he could find, leaving my own nerves frayed. Yet he had great tactile and auditory defensiveness. The sensation of grass under his feet, the sound of a dog barking, the echo of a public bathroom, would all send him screaming. And he never slept.

While Ethan made steady gains with language and was even hyperlexic, Daniel took a very long time to acquire expressive language. And I am still teaching him to read with fluency. Particularly because homeschooling has allowed him to learn at his own pace, Ethan's challenges are latent, and he has gained enough social skills over the years to function well among his peers. Danny, however, has remained very solitary, singular, with little inclination to build friendships. It has been painful to watch the gap widen developmentally between my sons, born a mere 21 months apart.

What of God's grace, so evident at first, then hidden, so as to require a deliberate effort to recognize it? Has he been less beneficent toward Daniel than Ethan? Had we exhausted his favor with Ethan? In light of the disparity between my sons' development, can we as parents say with as much confidence that God, "doeth all things well"? My husband and I concluded, yes. There has been consistent evidence of the Lord's grace upon and through the lives of both boys. Ethan's quick recovery was as an infusion of grace and met us gently at our level of theological maturity. Our early experience with Ethan was our Ebenezer— our marker of God's help (I Samuel 7:12, NIV). It built our faith and trust in God. But author Paul Tripp says of God, and the sort of grace we have experienced with Daniel, "There are many times when we are going through those kinds of things and we cry out, 'Where is the grace of God?' All the time, however, we are, in fact, receiving the grace of God. But it's not the grace of relief nor is it the grace of release…[it] is the grace of refinement." With Daniel, it has been the grace of persevering faith, of contentment with small victories, of steadfast love and daily mercies. Slow and even, it has been maturing grace, which has tested and stretched our faith.

Author Dietrich Bonhoeffer notes of Christians that, so often, "We pray for the big things and forget to give thanks for the ordinary, small (and yet really not small) gifts." It is a strange thing to say, and one in the thick of meeting the needs of a challenged child may disagree, but many years in, we can say that autism has been a gift to us. It has been a means to greater spiritual maturity, and there have been lessons in this crucible that may not have been learned otherwise. Over the years, the experience of raising children with special needs has caused us to reexamine our notions of who God is and what his grace truly looks like in the lives of his children. We have discarded the notion that the God-directed life is free of suffering, and we have come to accept his sovereignty over all that occurs, including adversity. While we still pray for Daniel's healing, this understanding has freed us from the belief that healing is the only evidence of the Lord's good gifts to us and to him. God's grace comes in the manner that will best accomplish his purposes in the lives of his children. With both of our boys, we have come to trust that the Lord, as Charles Spurgeon put it, "is more present than friend or relative can be, yea, more nearly present than even the trouble itself".

Discussion Questions:

1. How has God's response to your prayers on behalf of our children surprised you?

2. What areas or seasons of difficulty have you faced, which in hindsight you can recognize as blessings and grace in disguise?

3. How can you begin a habit of daily giving thanks in all things concerning your children to keep the perspective that God is near and active on their behalf?

Hey, This Is Fun!

DEBORAH ABBS

Be joyful always.

1 *Thessalonians 5:16, GNT*

Watching helplessly as Luke thrashed around on our much loved
and filthy office couch, Sarah, one of Luke's home therapists, and
I weren't sure what was upsetting him. Typically he loves this
worn piece of furniture—throwing off the back cushions and
burrowing down are great fun for him. But this time, not so much.
Besides the thrashing, he was crying and yelling.

From across the house I hear feet flying across the floor
and in runs Brandon, his older brother, catapulting himself over
the arm of the couch towards Luke.

"What's the problem, bro?" asks Brandon getting up in
Luke's face. "No need for all this crying!"

And then Brandon just starts being goofy, which can be
tough for a cool teenager to do.

Before I could tell Brandon to stop and not get super
close to Luke in case he started to lash out (Luke can be
aggressive when he is upset), Luke gets a huge grin on his face and
starts laughing. Just like that the meltdown, the sadness, turned to
joy! And Brandon and Luke spent a good twenty minutes goofing
around and giggling after that. It was a sweet, special time. Of
course I tried to take pictures, but as usual they didn't turn out

great. I am not known for my photography skills. More giggles and surprise happiness comes when Jessie, one of Luke's home therapists for many years now, arrives. She just has a way of teasing Luke and making him crack up that makes us all smile.

Another unexpected joy has come to us through Joni and Friends Family Retreat. In 2010 my friend, Carrie, talked about this family retreat being an awesome time for her family, and she encouraged us to attend. We had our doubts. The closest location for one of the many retreats held over the summer was in Michigan, and the camp was put on by the Joni and Friends Chicago office. How would Luke do with a four-hour car ride since he hates sitting and being hemmed in? *If this is for families that have someone with a special need in it, will I have any fun,* Brandon wondered? Mike, a big workout guy and healthy eater wanted to know what the food served there was like and if there was a workout room. I wondered how Luke would do with his short-term missionary (STM), assigned to him. Would he like this person who would essentially become a part of our family and help him for five days? And so it went.

Our worries turned to joy though when we pulled up to Maranatha Bible Camp where the retreat was held that June. When we pulled the car up to the door of the main lodge a Joni and Friends volunteer came out and asked us how we would like to be welcomed by everyone inside (quiet, medium, or loud), and then shooed us in, parked our car, and unloaded all of our stuff into our room. I was astonished first off that we were welcomed so warmly and that Joni and Friends staff and volunteers were sensitive to the fact that some folks with special needs are overwhelmed by loud noises. After that we had some time to get settled before dinner was served and we met Luke's STM for the week. Now Luke is always on the go, rarely keeps his shoes on, loves chips and lots of food, but typically eats on the run. I was nervous about his ability (or lack thereof) to sit in the dining hall, and I didn't know if he'd like the food, so I brought a big can of Pringles chips with us. Right away Luke's STM told me not to worry. And then a few tables away I saw a boy who looked a couple years older than Luke, and he was also holding a can of Pringles and had bare feet! That relaxed me so very much. We were just a part of the regular crowd there. Someone running around? Someone taking off their shoes in a restaurant? No biggie. We later met Quin and his family, and became fast friends that week.

Besides all that, Mike and I got a big break from our tag-team parenting—meaning one of us "mans" Luke while the other runs errands, takes a break, or visits with extended family and friends. With our STM to help, we could both sit and listen to sermons and have a date night while the kids did other fun things.

We've been back every year since and can't imagine not going every June. Brandon has a ball too, and he sees that he isn't the only sibling of someone with special needs. He's even gone zip lining, tubing, and horseback riding along with the rest of us. Mike and I have made good friends there who we get to see every year and some of them we see much more often. We had to go all the way to family retreat in Michigan to meet the Clark family, and it turned out that they live in the same town! They have become like family to us.

We've also been blessed to have the same STM, Stephanie, the last four years at family retreat, and she too has become a dear part of our family. Only someone who loves Luke a lot would join him on the beach in cold Lake Michigan like she does! At family retreat she, and the short-term missionaries for all the other families, truly become Jesus' hands and feet, and we get a much-needed respite. What an unexpected joy this was for us that first year and it continues to be a special, joyful time for us year after year.

The wonderful, unexpected couch incident, as well as thinking about Joni and Friends family retreats, got me thinking. It's natural for me to be on guard. Ask anyone living life with a child on the spectrum, and they will agree. I am poised for the next problem, or meltdown, or issue to arise at any given moment. But am I at all expecting or looking for the joyful, fun moments, like Brandon and Luke's time together that day or time spent at family retreat?

Brandon came in to help Luke because he loves him. Yes, it's a love-hate relationship. Yes, it is hard on Brandon having a brother that can't talk and interact in the typical way. But he was able to turn a tough time into something fun just by showing up and being his wacky self.

Jesus showed up on earth for us. He came to us and died for us because he loves us. Am I showing up where and when He wants me to? Am I looking for ways to turn "bummer, man!" moments into "Hey, this is fun!"? If I'm honest, not nearly as much as I should be. But I can pray and ask God to help me do this and for eyes to see these precious moments when they make an unexpected appearance.

Discussion Questions:

1. Am I expecting and looking for God to bring joyful moments and times into my life and the life of my family? Why or why not?

2. Do you have a special time like this that you can share with someone else to encourage them? If so, go for it! If not, ask God to help you see these times in your life.

3. Are you "showing up" where Jesus wants you to be? Are you loving others and sharing Jesus? Why or why not do you think?

Setting Our Watches to Reservation Time

KELLI RA ANDERSON

Hold on to what is good ...

1 Thessalonians 5:21b, NIV

I wasn't sure I had heard our family counselor, correctly. "Say that again?" I asked.

"Have you heard of 'reservation time'?" he repeated in response.

I shot a blank look at my husband who was sitting on the couch next to me in the small upstairs office. I had no idea what our counselor was talking about. After a solid hour of discussing the latest manifestations of Asperger-induced family trauma, I was just so tired I couldn't think straight. Or, apparently, hear straight, either.

"The Navajo have a custom," he explained, leaning forward in his chair. "Some families live miles apart without telephones. So, rather than show up unannounced on a neighbor's doorstep, visitors drive their cars within hearing distance on their neighbor's property. They park, and wait patiently for the neighbor to recognize their presence and give them the time they need to prepare their home. Eventually, the homeowners open the front door to signal they are ready to welcome their neighbors inside. Some call this kind of flexible living 'reservation time'."

Our therapist, Steve, paused and waited for my husband and I to connect the dots. From my husband's knowing nod, it seemed he already knew where this was going, but after a few loud ticks from the clock on the wall, I wasn't so sure my IQ was up to the task.

And then I got it.

All evening we shared our frustration and mounting fear about our nineteen-year-old's failure to launch. Despite transition programs, medication changes, and strategies tried-and-true to move this bright guy forward in his life, he still struggled so hard with poor executive function, organization, and motivation. As a result, he kept quitting jobs, had only passed one college class in two years, and was still living at home. So much potential seemed to be going to waste while we waited. And waited. And wondered. Was he ever going to launch? Was he ever going to be ready? Would he ever be able to live on his own? Would he ever open his front door to welcome adulthood and independence inside?

We wanted assurance. We wanted our son's life to go according to some kind of timetable that made sense. But there is no such thing with autism. And so our counselor nudged us to practice patience and grace, sitting in our metaphorical car, waiting for our son (not us) to determine when he's ready to open his front door to welcome adulthood inside. Like so many things in the world of autism, there is no timetable that we can set our clocks by. Reservation time. We must simply wait until our son tells us he is ready and the time is right.

Only, I hate waiting. I'm terrible at it.

Over the years, measuring milestones, achievements and development according to the timetables doctors, educators, and our own expectations created, we witnessed our son succeed fabulously in some ways and struggle painfully in others.

As he grew older, and the difficulties became more apparent, we grieved. We worried. We prayed. We wondered how much was a result of our own blundering mistakes as novice parents? How much was ASD? And what we could do to improve either?

We often felt so helpless, like bystanders, watching the pain our son experienced, sometimes manifesting itself in forms of self-harm, as he tried to finish school, learn self-calming strategies, self-awareness, and self-control. All so essential to navigating a happier life. There were times we had to face the fact that some milestones simply would not be met, while others might be, perhaps just not in the expected way or the expected time.

Over the years, he has worked hard to meet the challenges (and believe me, how we have celebrated!), while some of his developmental life goals are still very much a work in progress.

Now, almost twenty years old, our son has accomplished some amazing things, in his own way and in his own time. For example, we wondered if he would overcome his fear that bordered on near-paralysis about driving a car. But today, after enrolling him in a private driving course, he is one of the best drivers his age: very deliberate, careful, and focused. (We have since taken an unofficial family poll and agreed he did not inherit his driving DNA from his mother.)

At several points, we thought he might never walk with other graduates to accept his high school diploma, when anxiety became so toxic we feared he might have to be removed from school altogether. Then God led us to another high school, better equipped for students with spectrum disorders, enabling him to finally, in his fifth year, toss his mortar board in the air with 900 other high school graduates, completing his secondary education..

And now, we wait for the reaching of another milestone: his transition into adulthood. Will he be able to navigate the educational system he needs to train for a job? Will he be able to hold a job? And will he be able to live on his own, independently? What form will any of these things take? And how long?

We don't know. Reservation time. We must wait. Patiently. Prayerfully. Accepting what was, is, and whatever will be as right according to God's timing and God's purpose.

That, of course, is pretty hard to do for someone like me, who has never really hit my own milestone of maturity -- waiting without worry. I knew intellectually that our counselor was right, but my heart just wouldn't listen.

The next morning, curled up in my favorite corner chair, I opened my Bible to finish my reading in 1 Thessalonians 5:17-22. And there it was. The answer my heart needed to hear: "Hold on to what is good" (verse 20b).

How do I stop champing at the bit of my own impatience and my cookie-cutter hopes and let my son develop at his pace to achieve what he can as God allows? Hold on to what is good. The apostle Paul wrote these encouraging words to my struggling brothers and sisters in the persecuted church in Thessalonica to free them from their fear, just as much as God was writing them to me in our struggles to free me from mine. Hold on to what is good.

I need to keep my eyes turned away from what discourages me or causes discontent (1 Thessalonians 5:22). I need to pray with thanks to God, grateful for the good things I see even in the middle of difficult circumstances (5:17-18). And I need to ask the Holy Spirit to give me spiritual eyes to trust and celebrate with thanks what my own eyes cannot see during those same troubles (5:19). When I do these things, then I am able to wait in the parenting car, at peace, knowing that my son is preparing in his own way, in his own time, because his life and his purpose belong to God.

A few days later, being more purposeful to practice Paul's admonition to be thankful for God's work (seen and unseen), I stopped my inner grouch from grumbling about an ongoing, irritating problem with my son's transition-training program. Instead, I turned my prayer in a new direction and asked God to allow my son's work that day to be a blessing, in spite of the program's flaws, and to help him to take one more step toward self-awareness and responsibility.

When he got home later that afternoon, I remembered my uncharacteristic prayer, and wondered, would God surprise me? I asked my son if he'd learned anything new at work. His face lit up with a smile and he recounted an amazing eureka moment of self-discovery. I think at that moment my inner grouch did a dance of joy.

My son is growing into adulthood at his own pace and in his own way. As his mother, I am finally learning to reset my watch and to wait a little more patiently for the front door of his adult life to open. Apparently, the right time has been reservation time all along.

Discussion Questions:

1. What are some of the milestones that you have celebrated in your son or daughter's life that were met in their own way and on their own time?

2. What are some of the good things in the life of your child you can hold onto as a reminder that God is at work in their life?

3. Is there a developmental goal that is a struggle for your child right now and maybe is causing you to fear its outcome? Try to begin asking God to give you spiritual eyes to trust; thank Him for the work He is doing in your child's life, His never ending (sometimes unseen) work in the life and good purpose of your child, the child He loves.

True Gifts

KEVIN O'BRIEN

Every good and perfect gift is from above, coming down from the Father of the
heavenly lights, who does not change like shifting shadows.

James 1:17, NIV

Can you remember the joy of Christmas morning as a child? The
expectation and wonder of it all? I remember waking up
ridiculously early on Christmas morning after a late night at my
grandparents' house for Christmas Eve. Bicycles and GI Joes
(both kinds—the 70s era large dolls and the action figures),
Shogun Warriors, and a BB Gun. To be perfectly honest, I don't
remember most of them as much as I remember the buildup.
Sometime around high school I lost the wonder of it, asking
instead for clothes, or better yet, for money because my mom was
clueless about the clothes I thought looked good.

We all love getting presents.

It's interesting being on the other side, waiting, not to get
presents, but to give them to my kids. It is wild to watch the
reaction of kids opening presents. The joy, the desire for the next
one, occasionally the disappointment. As I write this, it is four
days before Christmas. Last night my wife said that she couldn't
wait for this Christmas because of a couple of things that the kids
are going to get. She can't wait for their reactions and neither can
I. Our oldest has largely achieved that detached high school phase

of being somewhat above all of this. I think that he's going to be a bit surprised. Sierra is too young to have given up the wonder. Nathan, well, Nathan is the best of us all when it comes to presents, there can be absolutely no doubt.

It's been that way for Christmas and birthdays as long as I can remember. Nate cannot suppress what he is feeling—good or bad—about anything. Presents are no exception. He cannot dissemble and make you think that he is patiently waiting, or you got him the best thing ever when in fact he really doesn't like it. No, whatever Nate thinks, you are going to know. If it's great he exclaims with glee, grins as wide as he can, and poses for a picture holding the present up in front of himself. If the present is okay but not terribly exciting, the process is much quicker, and he's on to the next one.

We make it a point not to go overboard on birthday and Christmas presents. I have bouts of extreme discomfort coupled with a low grade and near constant angst over our highly consumerist culture. I worry about what I am teaching my children about needing stuff to be happy, to feel as if *getting* presents is the epitome of holidays and special occasions. Nathan's reactions are something of a barometer for me.

One Christmas, we got him a movie that we knew he liked. As soon as he opened it we knew that we had made a miscalculation. "That's the wrong present!" he loudly protested with no concept that he was making his mother feel bad, that it is not polite to say such things, or that he is supposed to be grateful that someone wanted to buy him something they thought he would like. Concrete thinker. Concrete problem. Concrete solution. Let the world know that this is not right. And I do not exaggerate by much when I say world. We thought that we solved

202

the problem by getting his older brother to trade DVDs with him: *Monsters Versus Aliens* for *Kung Fu Panda*. It seemed to work. The day went on; I seem to recall that it got better. At least we stopped the immediate crisis. And then it started. For the next several weeks Nathan decided that he needed to tell people that he got the wrong present. After the initial shock, we could laugh about it. When he tells grandma, who adores him and does a very good job of getting him to act appropriately, it's one thing. You can smile and have a laugh because it is delivered in such a matter of fact manner. The earnestness of—well, I don't know if innocence is really the right word, but you get the idea—is a bit humorous. But you have to know him.

It feels a lot different when he decides that he needs to tell the random clerk at the store, or the librarian, or someone at church—people who have no context or clue who he is, much less why he would be volunteering such information. It can get a bit embarrassing. Disheartening. And while there is no rational need to do so, you feel like you have to explain the whole story. What happened, and the fact that he has autism, so he's still obsessing in it two weeks later. Three months later. Occasionally over a year later. It's amazing how long things stick.

I wouldn't call it a grudge. Nate doesn't do that, not really. He is a happy kid who has very set ideas about how the world works. Apparently owning *Monsters Versus Aliens* was outside the bounds. Who knew?

The difference between Nate and me is that I can hide my disappointment. He can't roll with the punches or make someone think that the gift they thought was so great was indeed just that great. I can. All the while I am wondering what on earth they were thinking. This? Really? I got the wrong present!

At this point in my life my brothers are not going to swap presents with me. And it dawns on me that perhaps I am not so different from my son.

I'm going to go out on a limb and say that I am not alone. On my worst days I must admit to wondering if James 1:17 is true. Does God really give us good gifts? Perfect? Really? I don't think so. Have you really noticed what my son is going through, God? Do you really care? How is this child a good gift? My worst days. I love my son, let's be clear. But the stress and the anxiety and the sheer exhaustion of it all pile up. And I know that I don't have it that bad. I know people who have to deal with far worse things, far more taxing things.

But I said that Nate is the best of us at presents. The DVD episode was certainly not that. But the same honesty regarding that one gift is the reason he is the best. When Nathan turned nine or ten, we had a party with my family for him. He was opening presents, making out like a bandit, when he came to a specific present. The present that everyone in the room knew he was getting. The present he gets every year. This time was different.

Every year Nate gets paper and markers because he loves to draw. He draws so much that I occasionally wonder if I shouldn't plant a tree every year to make up for the ones that have been cut down to support his habit. Everyone knows he's getting them. Everyone knows that he loves them. None of us were prepared for his reaction.

The wrapping paper came off and I could hear the smile on his face even though I was standing behind him. He read the label with glee, "Plain white paper! My favorite!" Yes. You read that right. A ream of printer paper. One with a label that literally read "plain white paper". I think that everyone in the room about died laughing. I almost wept.

The truth is that Nathan is a gift. A gift unlike any I could have imagined. I'm not much for surprises, but sometimes the best gifts are the ones that surprise. The ones that don't cost a lot or come in fancy boxes. They're not a car with a bow in the driveway on Christmas morning or the latest, hottest whatchamawhosit. They aren't things at all. Read the entire first chapter of James and you'll get an entirely different sense of what is important and what a good and perfect gift might look like.

Our wants and desires change, they shift like shadows. What we want one minute is not what we want the next. Most of the time we don't even know what we want. We need to learn to trust our Father of heavenly lights. To see that the gifts he gives are the best kind. He is the one who redeems us in our imperfections. Who uses the very things that are our weaknesses to confound the wise (and us, I might add). Who shows us what he can do with our imperfections and those of our autistic children.

My other children love their presents (mostly). But neither of them can hold a candle to Nathan's wonder. He is brutally honest. He can be embarrassing in his reactions in front of strangers. And then you get hit right smack between the eyes with the two by four of "Plain white paper! My favorite!" And you realize that the best gifts are not the ones you thought they were.

And that is why Nate is the best at getting gifts. (Just wait 'til he sees the Lego mug!).

Discussion Questions:

1. Do you view your child as a gift from God?

2. How can you view your child's weaknesses as a gift instead of a curse?

3. What kind of gift can you offer to others through their interaction with you and your child?

AFTERWARD

Keep On Keeping On: Continuing Our Faith Journey and Parenting

We all have struggles. I certainly do. Let's be honest; imperfection, cheating on diets, losing our parenting patience with an adult temper tantrum display, and the guilt that follow are just the human condition. Nobody is perfect.

Some people may blame their foibles on forces of evil (hence the mantra: "The Devil made me do it.") But me? I blame *Antiques Roadshow*. One evening this past month, I was so riveted to the TV screen I didn't hear my fifteen-year-old daughter talking to me from her perch on the stairs. It wasn't until after a collector's Chinese-carved rhino-horn ceremonial cup appraised at over a million dollars that I heard my daughter's cry break through the announcement. "You never listen to me!" she shouted. I turned toward her just in time to hear her footsteps stomp to the top of the stairs and fade away.

I turned and asked my husband, "What did I do?"

"You honestly didn't hear her tell you about school today?" he asked, incredulously. I turned back to the TV screen, now drawn to the image of a rusted Civil War-era sword and a rather large, dirty, clay pot. I wanted to know what they might be worth. I wanted to stop feeling guilty for just having blown a very important parenting moment. I wanted to blame *Antiques Roadshow* for its hypnotic power over my mind. But the truth is, TV is just one of many things lately I have allowed to distract me from interacting with my family.

Whether it's admitting that we have an addiction to PBS, that we are struggling with anger, with God, or something we'd rather not admit in public, the truth is that no person, and certainly no parent, can be perfect. From losing patience to losing perspective, the life of a special needs parent is difficult. But ironically, that is also our blessing because we, perhaps more easily than most, can also admit how much more we need God to help us, comfort us, guide us, and forgive us.

"...for all have sinned and fall short of the glory of God," the writer in Romans 3:23 tells us (NIV). God is not surprised by our shortcomings, sins, and imperfections. In fact, Scripture tells us that when His first children chose to disobey Him in the Garden, it resulted in a great divide between humanity and the Father. Everything comes with a cost and the cost of spiritual rebellion, or sin, was spiritual death.

"For the wages of sin is death," the writer echoes in Romans 6:23 about our universal human condition (NIV). And contrary to popular opinion, sin isn't just those behaviors that land us in jail. Sin is anything that has ever caused us to live short of the perfection and glory of God.

Thankfully, our story doesn't end with bad news.

"...but the gift of God is eternal life in Christ Jesus our Lord," the writer concludes in verse 23.

2,000 years ago, God stretched His arms wide to give humanity a gift we could never obtain on our own. Jesus offered His perfect life as a sacrifice in exchange for ours; He paid the ultimate price God did not want the rest of us to pay. And for those who accept His gift—an exchange of our imperfect personal histories for His perfect one—death will never be the end but only the beginning of a resurrected and eternal life.

Some of us have done this very thing—accepting and believing in Christ—so long ago as children that we barely remember. Others of us came to Christ later in life as teenagers or young adults. But if you are among those of us still undecided or perhaps someone who never really had it explained, let me assure you it is never too late.

And neither is it too complicated. Yes, a degree in theology comes in mighty handy for some. And twelve years leading to catechism might be helpful for others. But God is so good at keeping it simple; He only looks for a sincere heart. Like the thief on the cross, crucified next to Jesus, who had only to say, "Remember me when you come into your Kingdom," we, too, can come to Him and simply say, "Yes." Yes, we all have blown it. Yes, we all have been imperfect parents. Imperfect people. And yes, we want a relationship restored with God through Christ's gift of forgiveness. And like that young man whose last breath said yes to Christ's gift of mercy, we, too, can hear Christ respond, "Today you will be with me in paradise" (Luke 23:42-43, NIV).

If your faith journey is only just now beginning with a yes to Christ, let us, as fellow parents of special needs children who have contributed some of our faith journey in the pages of this book, be the first to welcome you into a very special family. If you are unsure where to begin this new life in Christ, let us encourage you to start reading one of the Gospels (Matthew, Mark, Luke or John) and to find community, support, love and growth in a local Christian church.

But whether you are a new believer in Christ or more mature in your faith, we, as parents of children on the spectrum, are all together on a special journey. We hope these vignettes have helped you know that you are not alone on this road. We are with you, and more importantly, God is with you.

It's our hope that just as you continue to grow in your journey caring for your loved one with special needs you continue to grow close to the God of the Bible. May God's blessings become ever more evident as you continue your new life in Christ!

Blessings to you,

Kelli

About the Authors

Deborah Abbs

Deb, who graduated from University of Illinois–Champaign/Urbana with a degree in journalism, works as a freelance blogger, as well as a disability ministry coordinator for InterVarsity Christian Fellowship in Illinois and Indiana. Her writing has been featured in several magazines and she was a columnist with the *Kane County Chronicle*. She currently contributes to Key Ministry's blog at www.keyministry.org/specialneedsparenting.

Deb received a certificate for completing the Beyond Suffering Course run by Joni and Friends International and is one of the administrators of the largest online special needs ministry leader forum, with over 1,000 members. At her home church, www.chapelstreet.church, she facilitates a book study for moms of children with special needs.

She lives in Batavia, Illinois, with her husband, Mike, their two sons, Brandon, 18, and Luke, 14, plus a crazy English bulldog named Crystal. When not otherwise occupied you will probably find her with her nose buried in a book. Her personal blog can be found at www.morethantalk.wordpress.com

Kelli Ra Anderson

Kelli Ra Anderson is a freelance journalist, speaker, author and award-winning blogger. Her articles on faith, autism, marriage and parenting have appeared in Christianity Today's *Leadership*

Journal, Today's Christian Woman, and Focus on the Family. She has been a featured speaker on Moody Radio and at various seminars. Passionate to help the Church embrace the gifts and essential role of all God's people, she founded and administrates the largest online forum for special needs ministry leaders, now merged with Key Ministry. (See Facebook, "Special Needs and Disability Ministry Leaders".)

Her memoir-devotional, *Divine Duct Tape,* (2012), explores a life lived in the daily tension of faith, parenting, and autism. With honesty and humor, readers are invited into a personal dialogue with God, asking our tough questions, discovering unexpected answers, and realizing God's ultimate desire is not the picture-perfect Christian life, but a life lived in harmony with the One who truly knows us, loves us, and is with us, every step of the way.

Kelli and Adrian, married 28 years, have three children, two of whom have special needs. They live in the far western suburbs of Chicago, Illinois.

KEVIN O'BRIEN

Kevin O'Brien is a husband, father, ordained minister, writer and volunteer theologian. He holds a Master of Divinity and Master of Theology from Liberty Baptist Theological Seminary where he won the Th.M. award in 1997. He has also done graduate work at the Institute for Christian Studies in Toronto. He is currently a brand manager on the Bible team at Tyndale House Publishers. During his time at Tyndale he has helped to develop several Bibles and has written articles which have appeared in *The Way,* the *iShine Bible,* and the *Illustrated Study Bible.* He also wrote a series of devotionals for WAYFM's World's Biggest Small Group and is currently at work on a devotional series and several unfinished novels which WILL be finished someday.

Kevin lives in the far western suburbs of Chicago with his wife, three children, a dog, and a cat. He would prefer to spend his time reading, writing, woodworking and watching the Chicago Blackhawks.

KATHLEEN DEYER BOLDUC

Kathy's son, Joel, who has autism, has been the inspiration behind her writing/speaking ministry for twenty-five years. It is her heart's desire to minister hope to other parents who are traveling the journey with disability. Kathy's published work includes *The Spiritual Art of Raising Children with Disabilities* (Judson Press), *Autism & Alleluias* (Judson Press) , *A Place Called Acceptance: Ministry with Families of Children with Disabilities* (Bridge Resources), and *His Name is Joel: Searching for God in a Son's Disability* (Bridge Resources).

She has a master's degree in Religious Studies from The College of Mount St. Joseph. As a spiritual director, and owner, with her husband, of Cloudland, a contemplative retreat center in southwest Ohio, Kathy creates a safe space for believers to explore and deepen their relationship with God. Contemplative prayer and Lectio Divina (sacred reading of Scripture) have been transformational on her journey as the mother of a son with autism. Her blog can be found at www.kathleenbolduc.com, as well as at www.specialneedsparenting.net

RICK AND MICHELE BOVELL

Michele and Rick are parents to five adult and teenage sons,
including two on the autism spectrum. In addition to his career as
an IT professional, Rick is ordained to the preaching ministry and
has served for years in church leadership. As a family, the Bovells
volunteer with various disability ministries, including Joni and
Friends—speaking, writing, and serving as short-term
missionaries--both in Africa and in the US. Currently, Rick and
Michele minister in local group homes, sharing Christ's love with
adults with intellectual disabilities and helping them do what they
are designed to do: worship the Lord.

BARBARA K. DITTRICH

The mother of three children, all of whom have a variety of
chronic illnesses or special needs, Barbara Dittrich founded
Snappin' Ministries (Special Needs Parents Network) in 2002
prior to its merge with Key Ministry in 2018. In October of
2009, Snappin' was one of three finalists for World Magazine's
Hope Award for Effective Compassion in conjunction with
the American Bible Society. With a unique vision for serving
parents of children with chronic illness, disability, or special
needs, she led her team in developing an innovative parent
mentor curriculum. She lives with her husband of over 25
years in Southeastern Wisconsin, writes and speaks
nationwide, and has contributed to a number of blogs since
2002. Barb also opines on her personal
blog www.barbdittrich.com.

214

MICHAEL ABBS

Mike Abbs, who graduated from University of Illinois-Champaign/Urbana with a psychology degree, has been a police officer for 23 years. Currently he is a police lieutenant, and he served on the SWAT team for 18 years. When his wife Deb isn't asking him to write vignettes, he enjoys spending time with his family, eating healthy, physical fitness, playing fantasy football and watching old movies.

Acknowledgements

FROM DEB:

To the Lord for His work in my life—where would I be without You? In huge trouble that's where!

Luke, you were the inspiration for this book project. You have taught me so much! And to my wonderful and patient husband, Mike, who puts up with my almost daily frozen coke run, lack of cooking and never-ending ideas that, of course, involve work for him. Also, to Brandon, thanks for being such a good big brother to Luke and a wonderful son.

To my parents, Donna and Dan, for all your love and support since I was a wee one. To my in-laws, Alice and Don, for their encouragement and love. To my uncle and fellow writer, Lorin, thanks for all the adventures.

This book project took a lot of people to make it a reality! First, to my partners in crime once God gave me this initial idea—Kelli and Kevin. I couldn't have done it without you and I so appreciate you sticking with it.

To the writers who believed in this project and contributed their awesome writing pieces—Kathy, Michele, Rick, Barb and Mike. And to author and friend Diane Dokko Kim for writing the foreword for our book.

To ChapelStreet Church of Geneva, for supporting Luke so our family can be part of the community and attend worship. Special thanks to Bruce, Chris, Jaimie, Michelle D., Andrea, Kerry, Chris,

Noah and last, but certainly not least, Michelle F., who has been buddies with Luke since he was a little guy.

A HUGE THANKS to the people in the two or three villages I mentioned in "It Takes a Village", who have helped Luke and our whole family. I'm sorry I can't name each one of you and forgive me if I miss someone! Katherine aka Squid, Lizz, and Jessie, you have made up Luke's core team in our home over the years and I am so thankful for each of you.

I'm grateful for the Batavia School District, the Early Childhood Center especially Lisa, Jocelyn, Kelli, Korin, Terri, Jeni, Deb and Susan. To our Giant Steps family, with a special shout out to Elementary E, Yosemite and the Rec Center. You have taught Luke so much and loved him well for many years. Thanks to his bus team over the years, especially Susan, Ruth, KJ, Mike and BP. To Autism Home Support Services especially Cheryl, Sarah, Mandy, Corinne, Diane and Jason. To the many doctors that keep us going: Dr. Wyma, Dr. Hazel, Dr. Nolan and Dr. Hart.

And where would I be without my own dear family and friends? During my roughest times some of you, including my mom, have literally forced me out of the house. I wish I could thank many more of you but, man, this is already going to be a very long list!

Special thanks to my amazing friends: Diana, Meg, Amy, Nancy, Cathy, Jodi, Kevin, Michelle, Sharon, Joy, Leslie, Merrilee, Julio, Heather, Mark, Laura, Kelli, Janet, Cathy D., Jill, Kristin, Tim, Nicole, Mary Lee, Jacquie, Cindy, and Carlyle.

Thanks to my brother, Dan, and his wife Melissa. And to my "baby" brother, Don and his wife Julia. Thanks to my brother-in-law, Don and his wife, Kim. Thanks to my brother-in-law, Steve and his wife, Carrie. And to all my nieces and nephews, love you bunches: Katie, Jeremy, Tony, Elizabeth, Nick, Maggie, Tommy, Meredith and Teddy.

Thanks to my InterVarsity Christian Fellowship family-- especially Sandy Cook, Jane and Jeff Pelz, Phyllis Le Peau and Robert Burdett.

I must not forget to thank the Joni and Friends Chicago office and my Joni and Friends Retreat friends who are very dear to me and just get it. Special gratitude goes out to the short-term missionaries who have cared for Luke during family retreats, especially Steph, who has been with our family six times.

And finally, thanks to those on a similar journey who read this book—may God use it in your life to be an encouragement and bring you closer to Him.

FROM KELLI:

To my Heavenly Father, for the privilege of getting to do something I love—the joy and sheer fun of playing with words— thank you, for allowing me to use what I enjoy to share with others what You have done and continue to do: to redeem, salvage, transform and bless my life and those I love. Thank you, thank you.

Thank you also to my children, Sarah, John and David who know better than anyone how hard it can be to live with a mother whose office is their home and whose lives are often the subject of her writing. I can't thank you enough for allowing me to share some of our family's story—some of your very personal stories—in an effort to encourage others who are also traveling a similar life road. I love each of you very much.

To my dearest friend and encouraging, patient, pun-loving husband, Adrian, thank you for your willingness to be my partner these past 28 years, as well as my sometime editor, timekeeper, sounding board, moral compass, and voice of reason. Best of all, you have been a wonderful father and a godly man and have made me (a woman who once wondered if she could ever love a child more than her first cat) a better mother and have challenged me to be a better person.

To Deb, thank you not just for the many coffee hours of friendship during this process, but for the faithful persistence and hard work you have invested to make your vision of Life on the Spectrum a reality; thank you for the privilege of being part of this book's creation. And to Kevin, where would we be without all your professional wisdom, patience, and perspective that has kept us from giving up during an unexpectedly long, 4-year process?

And finally, I am thankful for the new friends and connections I have made with very talented writers, designers and editors because of this project: Kathy Bolduc, Diane Kim, Michelle & Rick Bovell, Mike Abbs, Ellen Vosburg, Jan Kotynski (for whose long-suffering prayers, friendship and talents I am especially grateful), Colleen Swindoll-Thompson, and Barry Smith. My heart-felt love and thanks to all who saw the value in bringing encouragement and hope to families like our own. God's sweetest presence be with you all.

FROM KEVIN:

No book is the product of just one person. This book more than most. I want to thank Deb for inviting me to be a part of this project. Both she and Kelli have been an encouragement to me in this process as a writer, as the parent of an autistic child and as one who truly believes that God does not give us more than we can handle—without him that is; on our own is a different story entirely.

It is to God first and foremost that I give thanks. For my ability to write, for my family, for Nate, and most of all because screwed up person that I am, he loved me anyway.

There are so many people to thank that inevitably you forget someone along the way. So I am sticking to the basics. I want to thank Village Bible Church (especially the Sugar Grove campus) for your love and support of my family and making us feel welcome no matter what – I know that many families with kids on the spectrum don't have that and we don't take it for granted.

Thanks to my pal Barry who encouraged me relentlessly along the way and did this amazing cover for us. Thanks to Ellen for a great job editing and for often keeping me sane in our discussions of all things Church, theology, and the craziness that is American Christianity.

I want to thank my family for their support and encouragement through these years, it means a lot. Most especially, to my parents, Richard and Carol O'Brien, who are there all the time, and whom Nathan loves completely. To Rick and Judy Martin, Grandpa Rick and Grandma Judy, who took Loretta in and showed her what real love and family looked like – and have now extended it on to me and our children. To their daughter, Jackie – without you, none of that would have happened. Thanks for loving Loretta enough to make her your sister and for loving us, especially your birthday buddy, Nate. To the rest of the family, my brothers and sisters, my brother-in-law, sisters-in-law and nieces and nephews, and all of the rest of you I just ran out of space to include, you're still in here. Thanks for accepting Nate (and us) on this wild ride.

To my other kids Connor and Sierra. I know that the road is not always easy. Know that mom and I love you both more than I can say. I am proud of the people that you are becoming. Your love and concern for others, especially your brother, (even when he makes that difficult) means the world to us, to him, and believe it or not to yourselves. Most importantly it is honoring to God.

To Loretta. Well, I finally have something published. After all of the fits and starts, weekends at the coffee shop or the library, here it is. Thanks for letting me chase this dream. Without you our home doesn't function. I love you.

To Nathan. I have no idea if you will ever read this or have a clue as to what you really mean to our lives. It doesn't matter if you do. I love you buddy. More than you can possibly know. God loves you too. You are his precious gift to our family and you are teaching us far more than you could know.

Sola Deo Gloria!

45582177R00128

Made in the USA
Middletown, DE
17 May 2019